The Blistering Morning Mist

The Blistering Morning Mist

A Memoir

Kathleen Weaver Kurtz

To Anne,
With my best wishes,
Kathie

RESOURCE *Publications* · Eugene, Oregon

THE BLISTERING MORNING MIST
A Memoir

Resource Publications
An Imprint of Wipf and Stock Publishers
199 W. 8th Ave., Suite 3
Eugene, OR 97401

www.wipfandstock.com

PAPERBACK ISBN: 978-1-6667-0949-0
HARDCOVER ISBN: 978-1-6667-0950-6
EBOOK ISBN: 978-1-6667-0951-3

07/16/21

To my mother,
Miriam Virginia Lehman Weaver

Your love created the foundation of my life,
and your prayers have followed me always.
My greatest sadness is that I cannot put this book into your hands.

We must read the past as the unfinished story that keeps us changing.

—PÁDRAIG Ó TUAMA, *IN THE SHELTER*

Contents

Preface

THE NARROW VALLEYS OF eastern Kentucky have a way of cradling the mist long after the sun has clarified each branch and twig of the mountaintop trees and every feather of the circling hawks. It's as if the water-worn rocks in the creek beds, the blackberry tangles, and the motionless leaves of the white-trunked sycamores along the creek bottom need extra protection, extra time before they are exposed to the brilliance of the sun.

The mist hides the larger world from view. Sounds carry far. Unseen birds singing, a dog barking, a car door slamming, disembodied voices—all bits and pieces of stories one can speculate about but not see. The mist invites imagination, teases and tantalizes, hints at what is yet unknown.

I love the mist but have no time to enjoy it this particular morning. I am inside where everything is visible—scrambled eggs, toast spread with blackberry jam made from our pickings along the railroad tracks, Fisher-Price people strewn across the golden carpet, lamplight holding the outside mist at bay. It could be any early September morning, but it isn't. My son Geoffrey's blue eyes sparkle in anticipation of the new adventure. He stands still just long enough for my husband Wayne to snap a picture. Then it is time to gather jackets and keys and to head out for Geoffrey's first day of kindergarten.

I open the front door where we confront the impenetrable white fog. I can barely make out the scruffy growth across the street, along the railroad tracks, but Geoffrey doesn't pause. He darts around me, proclaiming loudly for all the world to hear, "Out we go, into the blistering morning mist." I smile to myself at his expansive excitement and sense of purpose. I marvel at his trust in the unseen world and his eagerness to enter. There is something poetic and archetypal in his words, something that calls me to ponder deeper meanings.

❦

I, like Geoffrey, grew up cradled in misty valleys, my first three years in another narrow Kentucky valley and then the wide Shenandoah Valley of Virginia, with its rolling hills where cattle grazed or gathered under majestic old trees on hot summer afternoons, where blue-gray outcroppings of limestone punctuated green hillsides, and golden grain rippled in soft waves. Mist did not visit us there as frequently as in Kentucky, but the blue mountains defined the edges beyond which I could not see and mist often hung in their hollows or hid their ridges.

Mountains were not the only boundaries nor mist the only barrier to sight. My Mennonite community constructed boundaries also: not visible ones like the Blue Ridge and Allegheny Mountains, but rules and traditions that circumscribed our lives. These expectations separated us from the larger world just as surely as the mountains did and, like the mist, limited our vision. I heard sounds and glimpsed tantalizing shadows and images beyond my community's borders. Mist held the promise of far-off brilliance—life in the blazing sun. I imagined crossing boundaries and breaking through the mist to a different life. I sometimes pretended, but I never believed I could fully enter it. Pretending and dreaming were substitutes for what I assumed could never be.

As years went by, I watched others venture beyond our small world, never imagining that I would or could plant myself outside its safety. I admired and sometimes envied those who did. I learned early that no place could offer complete protection, but the familiar held a degree of predictability that comforted me.

Over time, my small world changed. It became less isolated, and unfamiliar parts of the world gained a measure of familiarity. I made brief forays beyond the mist, always to retreat, relieved to be back in familiar space where I knew who I was. I didn't belong in the larger world. There, I was always one faux pas away from being exposed as an awkward outsider.

But life has a way of breaking boundaries. Some people take one giant step across a boundary and are in a new world, but for me, boundaries disappeared gradually, until one day I looked around and realized that I was in a world much different, much larger than the confined places where I began. The mist that protected me had slowly burned away and I now stood in the sun. I had, slowly, without realizing it, grown into larger worlds.

Well into the writing of this book, I remembered the words of a song I heard years ago, "Baptized (Prodigal Daughter)" by Cate Friesen, that give poetic expression to my growth.

> I was baptized by this riverside
> I grew up longing for the sea
> I will take this clay from beneath my feet
> I'll build a boat to carry me

I find this a rich metaphor—taking the clay beneath my feet, the stuff of my life, to build a seaworthy boat. Boats are usually made of metal or fiberglass, in the past of wood or bark, but in this song, the writer takes clay, the unlikely raw material at hand, and uses it to construct her way into a larger world.

I took the clay of my life—the ordinary, lowly happenings of my days, the simple and solid support of my family and community, my own inner resources—and discovered in them all that I needed to grow toward the larger world I longed for.

This book had its beginning one day as I sat with a client in my pastoral counseling office. "My life has not turned out anything the way I wanted it to," she said in despair. I tried to maintain a therapeutic expression of sympathy. I did feel the sadness she was carrying, but in that moment, I had a new realization: my life was much richer than I ever imagined it would be. In the following days, I kept returning to my new insight. I realized that I had a story I wanted to tell.

There are many stories I could tell about myself—my life as a wife, mother, and grandmother; my life as a gardener or cook or potter. Hints of those show up, as they must, in any recounting of events, but they are not the theme I have chosen, perhaps because they are not the areas in which I struggled the most. They are the roles that didn't stretch my imagination. What has surprised me is the work that has taken me outside of my comfortable picture of myself, the work that has called me to move into larger spheres for which I had few role models. My story is a universal one of growth from the small world of childhood to a much larger, more demanding, challenging, and complex world. But its particulars are mine. They illustrate how one girl, born into a unique community in the mid-twentieth century navigated her world. I am deeply aware that it is a story of privilege—a white, middle-class life in the United States—and I want to acknowledge that there are many whose struggles to achieve are beset with much greater challenges than those I faced.

I offer you, the reader, stories about the specific clay beneath my feet and how it has enabled me to travel to a more spacious world—a journey of discovering grace and growth in places I least expected to find them.

Acknowledgments

HOW CAN I NAME, let alone thank, all those who have helped me in the writing of this book? The ones mentioned below are only a handful of those who have contributed time, attention, expertise, and love.

First of all, thank you to Wipf and Stock, who saw enough potential in this book to be willing to print it, and to Matthew Wimer, who graciously guided me through the process of turning a manuscript into a book. Thanks also to all the others who helped at various stages along the way.

A big thank you to Jennifer Seidel whose editorial skills have wrangled the manuscript into shape and who offered gracious, tireless support in light of all my never-ending questions. Thanks also to Evie Miller who helped me think about parts of my story more clearly, who took time to talk in the midst of her own busy writing and publishing schedule, and whose strong friendship supported me and saw in me things I could not yet see for myself.

I owe much to my grandmother, Myra Lehman, and my mother, Miriam L. Weaver, who filled my childhood with stories and participated in the creation of many more. Their letter writing provided a reliable window into the past—two filing cabinet drawers full of two- to three-page single-spaced, weekly or biweekly letters typed on onionskin paper spanning my lifetime.

After Mother's death, her cousin Rosa Mae Kurtz Mullet offered me vivid, detailed information about life in Kentucky during the few years my parents lived there.

My two sisters, Carol Ann Weaver and Dorothy Jean Weaver, shared many childhood experiences with me and have added their memories to mine. Each read through an earlier draft of this book and made helpful suggestions, as well as cheering me on all along the way. Two more loyal sisters would be hard to find.

I have participated in several writing groups. The first, a Lifelong Learning group in Manassas, was led by Mary Winsky. Her love of good writing was infectious. She encouraged us to look beyond the surface words to the meanings we wanted to express. The participants of this changing group are too many to name, but you know who you are. Thank you.

There is also my clergy writing group: Lauree Hersch, Dana Cassell, and Cathy McCollough. Lauree eagerly began the venture of writing with me, offering her inimitable spirit and the kind of reflection only a former seminary professor could contribute. Dana, pastor extraordinaire, joined us, adding humor, unique writing skills, keen insights, and technical expertise. Then Cathy, a pastoral counseling colleague, joined us, bringing her professional expertise, social awareness, and support honed through years of shared history. Her Trader Joe's snacks got us through more than one lengthy conversation. These women, spanning six decades in age, spent an entire weekend focusing on my completed manuscript and helped me discern next steps.

My Harrisonburg writing group, Saloma Furlong and Esther Stenson, deserve medals and a whole brass band for the hours of combing through the nitty gritty details of commas and variant spellings as well as seeing the whole picture. They didn't let me get by with shortcuts and helped me shape this story into a more cohesive piece of work. Both of them, as published authors, gave me guidance through the process of getting this story into print.

A number of readers made their way through two drafts of my manuscript: Sandra Fox, Suzanne Doherty, Donna Burkhart, Mary Jane King, and Judy Lehman. They didn't allow friendship to get in the way of honesty and offered me invaluable insights and guidance. Special thanks to Mary Jane who, in a moment of my deepest discouragement, heard my voice amid a clutter of versions and encouraged me to cut away what wasn't mine.

My son Geoffrey, to whom I owe the title of this book, read the manuscript wearing his editor's hat and helped me tighten up the writing and cut unnecessary verbiage to which I easily fall prey. His insights have made this book stronger.

Alyson Campbell also read a draft, and her courageous forthrightness to her mother-in-law spurred me on to do my best.

My son Jeremy offered me ongoing interest and encouragement, asking frequently how things were going. He also played beautiful music to nourish my spirit.

To Miriam, Lewis, Ginger, Juniper, and Lennox—my five precious grandchildren—you have inspired me, sometimes requesting, other times demanding stories that required me to dig deep within my memory for unique details and to shape them into stories. You invited me to see myself through fresh, young eyes.

And finally, to Wayne who has been my rock, my support, my long-term partner in life—*thanks* is too small a word to use. Although you have had moments of uncertainty about some of my ventures, you have always been beside me, encouraging me, loving me, listening to me, and giving me a firm foundation from which to launch my flight. I could never have done this without you.

Part I

The Clay Beneath My Feet

With the mind you cannot penetrate that [mist] but with the imagination you can sense the presence that is actually there that you cannot see with the eye.

—JOHN O'DONOHUE, *WALKING IN WONDER*

1

My Birth

MY LIFE BEGAN ON Lost Creek, a narrow "holler" between folds of blue Kentucky hills, where hunting hounds bayed at night and mosquitoes hummed on summer days. It got its name from the creek that trickled over and around rocks—at times beside the road, at other times becoming the road. The sun beat down on Mother's mint bed. Noisy bees visited every flower. Tomatoes, beans, and corn flourished in the ribbon of bottom land, and blackberries clustered on thorny vines along the fence row going up the hill in front of our house. Pide (rhymes with hide), the cow, along with several horses—Dixie, Tipsy, and Topsy—roamed the hillside pastures. At dusk fireflies rose from the tall grass, and endless stars lit the summer nights.

In winter, drab leafless hills lay exposed to rain and snow. Roads stood deep with mud. Cold seeped through the cracks in the uninsulated walls of the house and settled into the bones. Wind rattled the thin window panes. Some mornings the bed covers sparkled with frost crystals, formed from the moisture of my parents' breath. When it snowed the world became briefly pristine and glittering before mud set in again.

Lost Creek was isolated, and little from beyond the narrow valley made its way in, except for its own boys returning from World War II. They looked for jobs that didn't exist and either left again or gathered restlessly with little to do. There were no telephones to connect them with the outside world, and battery-powered radios pulled in only one or two stations. Mail arrived sporadically at best. The twenty-mile drive to Paintsville took two hours for people like my parents who were lucky enough to have a vehicle. Going by horseback took even longer. The road began as little more than a horse trail, which followed the rocky stream bed, dipping and twisting. The tin-and-canvas box of a jeep my parents drove bounced over rocks, giving its occupants an uncomfortable ride. Eventually the road gave way to gravel construction, which seemed a relief after the rough beginning. The last four miles became a heavenly pavement that smoothly delivered its travelers into Paintsville. A trip there took the whole day. It involved stopping to pick up various people along the way and then waiting until everyone completed their business. It was often dark by the time everyone reached home.

Hillsvue Glen shortly after my parents moved there.

Paintsville itself was small and unremarkable. Years later it would have its moment in the sun when President Lyndon Johnson came there to declare his War on Poverty, but in the chilly November of 1946, it had not known a newsman's camera, let alone a presidential visit. It consisted of a collection of houses, a few five-and-dime stores, a Kroger grocery store, a drugstore, and a sprinkling of other shops. No superhighway came near, but trains ran through the town and provided its best link to the world beyond. In Paintsville everyone knew everyone else. My parents were outsiders who talked differently and dressed strangely. They stood out clearly but were treated with respect.

This was the small world I entered. Unlike our neighbors on Lost Creek, Mother traveled to town to a real hospital for my birth. Not wanting to risk waiting until labor began, my parents came early, and whiled away several days at Cox's Tourist Home, eating at the Kentucky Diner or the Slick and June Bug, and walking the few streets of town.

Paintsville's small, sparsely equipped hospital was lacking in basic sanitation. When my mother was admitted in the middle of the night, the nurse on duty didn't have a key to the storage closet, so my fastidious mother began her hospital stay in a bed with dirty sheets. Her private nurse, a family friend sent by my grandparents to be with her in this isolated place, observed a cockroach exploring a tray of "sterile" instruments. Mother didn't concern her family with these details. She simply wrote afterward that the hospital "lacked order and cleanliness." She did, however, spare no detail about my birth in her single-spaced, three-page, typed account.

Early in the morning after my arrival, Papa called his parents in Iowa. Then he called to Virginia, where my mother's parents were about to leave for a class reunion at their Pennsylvania alma mater, Millersville State Normal School. Being proud first-time grandparents, they were especially happy that the news came in time for them to be able to tell classmates about the new baby.

Twenty miles away on Lost Creek, Aunt Esther, Mother's sister who was living with my parents and teaching school, waited impatiently—as she had for days—hoping the evening mail would finally bring news of my arrival. She did not suffer well any news vacuum, and this one was particularly hard to tolerate. Here she was, nearer to her sister Miriam (my mother) than any other family member but farther away than California in terms of communication. Finally, on Friday evening the much-anticipated postcard arrived. She eagerly read its brief message written by Papa, as if from me, saying that I had arrived and that my "farther" and mother were doing fine. (Papa was never allowed to forget that misspelling and was called Farther Weaver for a long time afterwards.) The next morning Aunt Esther and several others who, like my parents were doing mission work with the Mennonite Church, made the bumpy trip to town, stopping on the way to pick branches of holly covered with red berries for my mother.

A few days later, when my parents took me home, Mother was both excited and scared. If something went wrong, she was two hours away from any medical help. She couldn't call her mother or any of her friends for advice, and once her nurse left, she was alone with me all day—alone in the sense that no one lived within sight or yelling distance.

❧

In my parents' families, people named houses, so they named theirs Hillsvue Glen. I imagine them as newlyweds, sitting on their front porch swing, trying out names as they looked across the creek to the hill rising beyond it, and I am sure it was Mother who came up with the name. It sounds like her. I can hear the lilt in her voice as she tries it out, and I can picture my adoring father agreeing simply on principle. It seemed that anything she did was remarkable to him because she had done it.

That our house had a name was not the only thing that set it apart from others. Typical homes on Lost Creek were small, dark, unpainted buildings with few windows. Most local people had no vehicles and, therefore, no way of bringing in materials from the outside, so they produced almost everything themselves. They cut timber from their own land and planed it into rough planks for the board-and-batten walls of their homes. Floors were usually one board thick, with generous cracks that allowed cold air to come up from the crawl space below, a space that served as a retreat for chickens, cats, and dogs. River rocks were used to build support pillars for the corners of the house and for the fireplace—the rocks held together with clay dug from the riverbank. Roofs were frequently made of split wooden shingles, and window and door screens did not exist. Fireplaces served for both heating and cooking.

Soft bituminous coal was plentiful and free for the digging, usually no more than three feet underground, so families dug a supply from their own land. The black smoke created by the fire saturated walls and ceilings, covering everything with a layer of soot. No one had indoor plumbing. Instead, people built crude outhouses over the nearest stream, trusting that the water would carry away the waste. Electricity was still in the future. Kerosene lamps provided whatever additional light was needed, but most people lived close to natural cycles, going to bed and getting up with the sun.

Our house had been built by someone who had moved away from Lost Creek. It was constructed of smoothly planed lumber, had painted siding and a metal roof, and came equipped with a kerosene kitchen stove. My parents covered their interior walls with building paper and then real wallpaper—not catalog pages like local people used. Although they were renters, Papa screened in the back porch and made door and window screens. Like other houses, it had a porch across the front, but ours boasted a wide wooden swing suspended on chains. Each room had one or two large windows. My mother scrubbed and painted the inside woodwork and the parts of the floor not covered by the linoleum they bought in town. Using the treadle sewing machine her parents gave as a wedding gift, Mother sewed printed feed sack curtains for the windows. The rooms looked fresh and new—a real "bride's house," her mother commented after her first visit.

Like their neighbors they had no electricity, but my parents did not expect to go to bed when it became dark. They sat close together, sharing the light of a kerosene lamp, my father reading or preparing a sermon, my mother typing. Sometimes, if the kerosene was low, Mother typed in the dark. Eventually they got a Coleman lantern, which seemed almost as bright as an electric light, my mother reported to her family back home.

To the neighbors, our house must have appeared fine beyond measure and my parents, people of unlimited resources. No wonder apples disappeared from the shed and horse feed from the barn. Sometimes packages "didn't arrive." If the local carrier suspected there was money in a letter it also "got lost." Neighbors borrowed frequently, anything from lard to hay, and often these items were not repaid. Mother fretted, not really understanding how resource-full she and Papa appeared. They had a nice house. They drove a car or jeep as well as rode horseback. They went to town to buy groceries that must have seemed luxurious to people whose main diet was cornbread or biscuits and whatever meat they hunted or raised and whatever vegetables were in season. My father described a generous company meal he was served at a neighbor's home—"corn bread, biscuits, green beans, fried and cooked potatoes, cabbage and coleslaw, eggs and coffee." In contrast, my parents had canned meat, vegetables, and fruit. They baked white bread and even sometimes made ice cream if they had been to town and could bring home ice. They bought things like tapioca and Jell-O and cocoa powder.

Mother looked at her life on Lost Creek through her outsider eyes and noted what didn't work well. The newly installed stove made the house warm after weeks of inadequate fireplace heat, but it puffed black smoke whenever the door was opened. The furniture and dishes took on a layer of black soot, and heat-induced shifts in the wall resulted in cracks and tears in the freshly hung wallpaper. Lack of running water made life more complicated, and even though she had a kerosene-powered washing machine, it took both of my parents to carry enough water to do the laundry. The nearest water source for washing clothes was iron-rich well water, which tinted Mother's new white sheets a yellowish orange in the first washing. After that, they carried water from a spring or caught rainwater. The outdoor pit latrine was a step up from most local outhouses, but it was a step down for Mother, who grew up with indoor plumbing. Eventually my father piped water into the kitchen and rigged up a drain to the outside. The neighbor children found this novelty fascinating. They ran laughing back and forth from the kitchen to the outside to see the water disappear from the kitchen sink and appear at the end of the drain pipe outside.

Mother's ability to feed me was different from that of her neighbors. I got a daily dose of vitamins and drank orange juice in a bottle as well as milk. I started eating vegetables and fruit. Mother noted that I was much more alert and active than neighbors' babies who ate mostly biscuts and gravy. She kept careful records of my weight and height, of when I could hold up my head, and the first time I turned over. She bathed me in the dining room in the warmest part of the day and began reading to me long before I could understand a word. She held me as much as she could, and in that way, she was like her neighbors. When she left me with one of them for a few hours, she never worried about my well-being because she knew that I would be held and given continuous attention the entire time I was with them. What they couldn't afford in terms of material resources was more than compensated for by attention showered on babies.

2

Backstory

MY PARENTS WERE TRANSPLANTS. Neither of them grew up in Kentucky. My father, Melvin Hershey Weaver, came from Iowa and my mother, Miriam Virginia Lehman, from Virginia, where they met and married. They were sent to eastern Kentucky by the Virginia Mennonite Mission Board to establish churches in this remote area and to offer other skills and services to meet the physical needs of the people. The latter was secondary. Preaching the gospel and "winning souls for Christ" were the primary focus.

They moved to Lost Creek several months after their marriage and "set up housekeeping" in Hillsvue Glen. Before I arrived, Mother often spent her days alone, keeping house with few modern conveniences, while Papa taught in a one-room schoolhouse, took people to town for groceries and medical care, and ground corn or sawed wood using a small gas engine. Together my parents visited neighbors and tried to develop friendships, responding to the needs they saw. Sundays they held services, often at one place in the morning and another in the afternoon or evening. This proved to be more than full-time work. Letters home were full of a tiring array of activities, including all those necessitated by lack of electricity, plumbing, and easy transportation.

Mother lived for the mail that came from home and thrived on visits from her mother, sisters, and various people from her home community. At one point she wrote home saying that she felt far from "civilization." It wasn't primarily electricity, running water, and paved roads that she missed. While these made a huge difference in her day-to-day life, the thing that she missed the most was the vibrant life of the college town

in which she had grown up and the surrounding Mennonite community where she had belonged in a way she never would in Kentucky. She
longed to be at home for choir programs and special events. She asked for
all the news from the college and eagerly read its weekly purple mimeographed newspaper, which her parents sent. She inquired about various
students and asked what kind of cake her mother made for the annual
student outing. She missed the visitors who came to her parents' home
and hungered for classical music. Instead of needing to choose which
music program or church service to attend on a Sunday afternoon or
weekday evening, she faced quiet evenings at home—no events to attend,
no close-knit community of which she was a part. Yet, most of the time
she was happy.

My parents' wedding portrait.

My parents were deeply in love and they reveled in each other's
company. They also had a deep sense of mission, feeling that God had

called them to this place, so they accepted the inconveniences and isolation as part of "the price to be paid" for answering God's call.

The "civilization" my parents came from was in many ways as separate and different from the larger world as Lost Creek seemed to them. Having grown up in insular communities themselves, it was difficult for them to step back far enough to gain a larger perspective.

My father was an Iowa farm boy, at home in the softly rolling hills and cornfields of southeastern Iowa and the "good old Iowa mud" he delighted in. When they were courting, he once wrote to my mother about a trip home from town in which he didn't touch the steering wheel for a mile and a half because the muddy road was so deeply rutted that the tires stayed in their tracks without any assistance.

My mother was daughter of the dean at a small church college in the Shenandoah Valley of Virginia. She loved the blue mountain ridges hemming in the farms and fruit orchards of "the Valley," as local people called it. The mountains rooted her in life just as the college provided the center for her social, spiritual, and intellectual life.

However, what defined both of my parents most completely was being Mennonite, descendants of eighteenth-century German-speaking Swiss Anabaptists who, at the invitation of William Penn, made their way to Penn's Woods, landing in Philadelphia and creating farms in the rich, wooded area to the west. They came seeking respite from the persecution they had experienced at the hands of the Catholic, Lutheran, and Reformed churches in Switzerland and Germany. They were well content to settle quietly on their new land, to work hard, and to worship together without secrecy. Everything about these people was simple and straightforward—their speech, their dress, their homes, their churches, their entire way of life. They were happy to live in limited contact with the outside world.

During the early decades of the 1900s, this intentional isolation began to break down. Children went to public schools, and some adults began entering professions that required higher education. Interest grew in developing schools that equipped young people for a chosen profession and offered education in the context of their faith. One of the greatest fears about education was that young people going off to secular colleges would lose their faith and the unique practices of dress and lifestyle that included a list of don'ts—no smoking, drinking, swearing, dancing, movies, card games, or gambling.

My mother's parents, Chester and Myra Lehman, were among those who believed in the importance of Mennonite institutions of higher learning. After years of schooling that included skating around "questionable" modernist and Calvinist theologies, Grandpa received a master's degree from Princeton Seminary. A week later he and Grandma married.

My grandmother had graduated from normal school (teacher's training school) and taught for several years in Pennsylvania, but once married she became a full-time homemaker. However, her interests were not limited to home. She read widely, kept up with politics, and had a keen interest in people and places. Her learning was broad and inclusive, while Grandpa's was focused on professional work.

In 1921 both Grandpa and his brother Daniel had been hired to teach at the newly established Eastern Mennonite School near Harrisonburg, Virginia, which at that time offered the equivalent of a four-year high school degree. Faculty members were expected to teach a range of subjects in those early days, but Grandpa's main focus would be Bible and theology.

The brothers and their wives moved together, bringing all their household goods loaded high on a single truck. Their sister Elizabeth already lived near the school. Her husband, John Kurtz, had built its first building and bought a parcel of land nearby large enough for houses for himself and his two brothers-in-law. Within a few years the houses of the three siblings, all built by John, stood in a row on an unpaved street that would later become College Avenue. "The School," as it was always referred to by the family, quickly became the center of their lives. For my mother, cousins abounded on their street, and those who weren't cousins were mostly children of other faculty members. A tighter community would be hard to find.

My mother and her siblings grew up with unquestioning loyalty—first of all to their faith and then to the School and the importance of higher education. Their home was filled with books and music. Students, educators, preachers, church administrators, and missionaries returned from foreign places visited, keeping the house alive with ideas and activities.

My father was one generation away from Virginia. His parents, Amos and Lizzy (Elizabeth) Weaver, moved from Virginia to Iowa months after they married. Their life revolved around the farm where Grandpa raised all kinds of fruit as well as grain crops and set up a combine business with his sons. He took great pride in their mechanical skill and efficiency.

Grandpa Weaver was a deacon in their church and took that role seriously, as did Grandma, who filled the expected role of a deacon's wife.

They attended Sunday services both morning and evening. No matter how busy they were with farm work, they always stopped in time for Wednesday evening prayer meeting. They attended meetings at other churches in the area as well and had many church-related visitors in their home.

Like Grandma Lehman, Grandma Weaver was a homemaker. She hadn't finished school until she was 19 because she enjoyed working in the fields during the fall and spring. In Iowa she was known for her hospitality, her bountiful garden, and her generosity. She taught her daughters how to bake, garden, sew, and clean. Her words were few but well-chosen and kind.

While school structured Mother's growing up and farming formed Papa's early life, it was the church that claimed the highest loyalty in both families. Each of their parents had begun married life by moving in response to the church's call, so it isn't surprising that my parents did the same.

My parents met as students at the School, fell in love, and became engaged just before their final year of study. That winter they were asked about going to Eastern Kentucky, where mission work was beginning. The area was poor and the needs great. To my idealistic, young parents, this seemed a call from God, which they gladly accepted. They moved to Kentucky to join another couple already there.

My parents worked hard to learn to know their Kentucky neighbors, who lived in a kind of poverty my family had never experienced. Most had not attended high school. Few had any books, with the possible exception of a Bible. Most were Hard Shell Baptists, and for them church meant emotional preaching and dramatic participation and responses. Their faith was a stark form of Calvinism that stated that when God wanted you to be saved, "He" would strike you down, and until that time came there was little an individual could do about it.

My parents came with good intentions. They hoped to share their faith with these fiercely independent mountain people and to help them live better in every way. They were not mistaken in seeing the area as a place of great need. But the local people were also right in being suspicious of these outsiders. My parents had an agenda. What they envisioned was a little colony that would look almost like the ones they left behind. My mother shuddered at the singing style in the local churches and could hardly sit through a sermon by a Baptist preacher, with its high-pitched cadence. It didn't occur to her or Papa that their own ways may have been equally difficult for their neighbors to appreciate.

When one or two women joined their church, my parents expected them to wear coverings: white net caps worn by Mennonite women after they became church members. Soon after she joined the church, one woman told my parents she was "giving up the covering" because her hair was a covering, "a well-worn argument," my mother wrote to her family in frustration. The woman's husband expressed reluctance to becoming a Christian and retorted, "Well, if I was to become a Christian, I sure wouldn't join the Mennonite Church." Mother reported that they heard from others that people didn't want my parents to talk to them any more about their spiritual condition. She described their coming home after long afternoons of riding horseback up into the little branches where people lived, feeling discouraged and like failures, sometimes wondering what they were doing wrong, but mostly feeling that people were "hardening their hearts."

Being pacifists, it was hard for my parents to connect with returning soldiers whose experiences differed vastly from their own. After the high drama of war, the narrow valleys, limited jobs, and lack of places to go felt stifling to these young men. They spent much of their monthly government pensions on alcohol and manufactured adventure however they could. Their search often brought them to the schoolhouses where my parents and their coworkers were conducting church services. In contrast to the lively Baptist or Pentecostal services, the Mennonite services— with their staid hymns and almost conversation-toned preaching—offered little excitement. The drunken young men did what they could to liven things up. Sometimes they came inside and heckled the preacher. More often they stayed outside and called in the windows or began fist or knife fights that slowly but surely drew the attenders outside either to observe or to escape the scene. On rare occasions someone broke a window. Once a person threw a large handful of grass through the window, which landed on my baby sister's face. On another occasion a drunk man attempted to ride his horse into the school building.

Until this point in their lives, my parents had probably never faced a drunken person. Neither the required "personal evangelism" class at the School nor the preaching course my father took included methods for coping with fistfights during the sermon or how to disarm a man with a knife. None of their classes dealt with cultural sensitivities.

My parents felt keenly the clash between their own culture and that of their Kentucky neighbors, but they had been given no framework within which to understand what they were experiencing. In that era few Mennonites asked questions about how to translate their practices into meaningful equivalents for people in different settings. Mennonite customs were seen as the right ones and should be universally applied.

In later years, Mother regretted their lack of awareness and wished they had approached people more openly. She wished they had lived among them without requirements, offering what help they could and working to understand rather than judge them for their differences.

My parents did form good relationships. A colleague reported that "people think Melvin has a good turn (disposition) and they like him but just don't believe the way he teaches." Neighbor children came to visit and often stayed for a meal. My father made himself available for help of many kinds. In return, neighbors almost fought for the opportunity of watching me and my younger sister when my parents needed to go somewhere, and they offered my family meals with true mountain hospitality.

Despite these challenges, Mother came to look back on her five years in Kentucky as the halcyon days of her life, the Camelot that existed for "one brief shining moment." They were the years she was happiest—the years when she was married, in love, and when life seemed full of possibilities for the future. All the stories she told us in later years came refracted through the sepia of a wistful nostalgia. That life sounded almost perfect to me, her young listener. It was the period of our family life against which all other times were measured and found wanting.

3

First Memories

I THINK OF MY earliest memories as brief, isolated snapshots surrounded by haze. As hard as I try, I cannot penetrate the unknown context around them.

Papa and Mama are frying potato chips and draining them on cut-open brown paper bags on the kitchen table. From my vantage point I can barely see the crisp edges of the tempting morsels, my eyes level with the tabletop. The allure is too great. Even though I had been warned not to touch them, I take one and burn my tongue. I know enough to realize that complaining would be telling on myself, so I suffer in silence.

I walk proudly down the dirt road with Papa, wearing new brown boots. I head straight into a large mud puddle where my boot sticks. I pull with all my strength and my foot slips out of the boot, leaving the boot in the mud. Frantically I burst into tears, knowing this new boot is lost forever. Papa, who by now has squatted down on his haunches to help me, throws back his head and laughs. I am puzzled at his response to this catastrophic event, but he easily frees my boot, and in that instant my world is righted.

Papa and I play a game. I stand on the garden hoe, one foot on either side of the handle which I grasp firmly. Papa lifts the hoe and lowers me into the creek so that the water runs over my bare toes. The water is cold and tickles. He lifts me out and then dips me again. I don't want him to stop.

Standing barefoot in Lost Creek.

On Sunday mornings we ride on horseback over a hill to Burchett's Flat for church services held in a schoolhouse. I am riding with Aunt Esther, who holds me in front of her as the horse picks its way down the rocky hillside. I fear the horse will slip and fall or that I will slide off as it descends, but Aunt Esther holds me tightly and explains that the horse is better able to walk around the rocks than we are—the horse will not fall. I wonder how she can state this so confidently. I almost believe her but relax only when we come to level ground.

The kitchen windows are steamed over and the room filled with the smell of oatmeal cooking on the stove. Mama adds raisins.

I need to keep a distance. The round black heater is too hot to touch and smells of kerosene.

On a spring night the high-pitched chorus of spring peepers fills the air, and on chilly fall nights, off in the hills, the hollow disembodied bay of hounds mean that men are hunting possums. I am safe in our house with Papa and Mama.

I sit on the wooden stool on our screened-in back porch as the western sky provides a moving picture of salmon and pink clouds. I am eating blackberries and bread soaked in milk, and Mama stands beside me. No one speaks, but we listen intently for the distant sound of the cowbell that signals Papa's return with the vagrant beast. I feel at peace, content, complete. There is nothing more I want, nothing more I need.

My small, mountain-constricted world was about to enlarge. The mission board, with input from my parents and their colleagues, decided that we should move to a place where their efforts would be more welcome. In August, several months before I turned three, we moved to a house trailer at Crockett, not far from Lost Creek. There were four of us now. Carol had been born a year and a half after me, and mother was pregnant again. It didn't take long to realize that the crowded, poorly insulated trailer would not be adequate for us through the winter, so in December we moved back to Harrisonburg, Virginia, to wait for the mission board to give my parents a new assignment.

4

Papa

THE AFTERNOON INCHED TOWARD its close. Gray clouds clustered high above, but no rain—just a windy March day. I heard an engine start somewhere outside and rushed to the window, hoping to see Papa's small plane coming in toward the airport at the edge of Park View. The sound was only from the generator in the shed behind our building, but I stood at the window and watched anyway, hoping I'd see the small speck in the sky that meant his plane was coming. He had been gone all day and I was eager for him to return.

Behind me in the kitchen, Aunt Dot put the finishing touches on our supper. She had come to help Mother, who was recovering from surgery and needed assistance with Carol, tiny baby Jeanie, and me. "Supper's ready," she called. "Should we go ahead and eat, or should we wait for Melvin?"

"I think we'd better eat," said Mother coming into the kitchen. "The girls are hungry and will soon be fussy. We can save some for Melvin for when he gets here." We went ahead, with Papa's place sitting empty. Maybe he would walk in before we were finished. We ate our golden home-canned peaches for dessert, and still he had not arrived.

Ever since December of 1949, we had been living in Park View, the village surrounding Eastern Mennonite College (The School had now become a college.) We rented the second floor of a big brick house just across Mt. Clinton Pike from the School, within easy walking distance of Grandpa and Grandma Lehman's house. I had just turned three and Carol was not yet two. We hadn't been there more than a few weeks when Jeanie, my youngest sister, surprised everyone by making her entrance into the world two months early. She spent her first month in a hospital incubator and was allowed to come home then only because Aunt Dot, Mother's youngest sister who worked as a nurse at the hospital, could look in on her every day. At the end of her second month, Jeanie was thriving but still tiny.

Living in Park View suited us well. We went often to Grandpa and Grandma's for meals. On Sunday mornings, Grandpa picked us up for church at Mt. Clinton Mennonite Church, where he preached. My parents had opportunities to visit with many friends whom they'd rarely had time to see on short trips home. For these few months, living was easier than in Kentucky—electricity, running water, central heating. Other than caring for us, my parents did not have many responsibilities.

Papa took advantage of his free time to learn Morse code in the hopes of becoming a shortwave radio operator. He also borrowed a wire recorder, precursor of the tape recorder, from Uncle Bob, Mother's younger brother. Recording was a novelty, and Papa enjoyed being able to play with the new technology. He had memorized a poem to give at one of the worship services during the ministers' seminar he was able to attend, so he recorded himself practicing it. I watched, fascinated, as he turned knobs, spoke into the strange contraption in his hand, rewound the wire, and then listened to himself speaking. Finally, not able to contain my eagerness, I came running toward him and blurted out boldly, "I wanna talk frough it." He smiled and held out the mic to me and said, "All right, talk," but I became selfconscious and couldn't think of a word to say. In panic I responded with a voice that literally faded away, "I can . . . I can hardly talk." I might have forgotten this incident except that, as recorders are wont to do, it recorded both my clear, strong-voiced request and my affected fading away, giving the lie to my excuse.

These were happy months for me because Papa was home more than usual. One morning I sat on the counter next to the kitchen stove watching Papa. He beat eggs, added milk, and sprinkled in cinnamon. Then he dipped slices of bread in the mixture and placed them in the black cast iron skillet, where they sizzled as they fried. As he worked, he talked with me about Mother, the new baby, and what we were going to do that day. I watched his quick movements with fascination. Mother always moved with deliberation. He was fast, and he was always cheerful. I loved being with him. My papa could do anything.

When Mother came home from the hospital, she was not to go up and down stairs, so Papa and Uncle Bob carried her upstairs on a little rocking chair. The rest of us trailed behind like a parade, happy and laughing. We laughed too one day when Papa sat on the daybed that we used as a couch and held Mother on his lap. She held me, and Carol sat on my lap. I liked being all together.

On another, less happy day, I rode my tricycle in the hallway between our living room and bedroom. Carol followed on her wooden kiddie car. I made a game for myself of inching the trike as close to the top of the steps as I could but, being older and wiser than Carol, told her she wasn't to copy me. She wasn't big enough. Of course, she took my warning as a challenge and rode her kiddie car to the edge of the top stair—and then beyond it, clattering down the wooden steps. Which was louder, her screams or the clatter of wood on wood, I'm not sure, but Papa burst through our living room door, ran down the steps, two at a time, scooped her up and carried her back upstairs in his capable arms. Bright red drops of blood clustered on her lip. I felt both guilty and terrified. I had never before seen a person's lip bleed and was certain that it meant she would die. I hovered guiltily on the fringes, waiting for her to fade away, but Mother consoled her and Papa got ice to put on her puffy lip. To my relief, she soon returned to her lively self. No one asked me what had happened, so I held my guilty truth. I knew I had tempted her by my example. I had failed in my responsibility as a big sister.

Supper was finished when we heard footsteps on the stairs. We must have missed hearing Papa's plane, I thought. Carol and I ran to the door eager to greet him, but it was Grandpa who opened the door. I don't remember his face, but Mother said one look told her the news. Papa wasn't coming home. Ever. I sat in my little orange rocking chair, rocking and rocking. I had no feeling. There was no reason left to feel.

Somehow, we all got taken down to Grandpa's house that night and went to bed there. Aunt Dot remembers hearing Mother crying in the night and Grandpa getting up to comfort her. At some point I came to Mother's bed saying I couldn't sleep, so she told me to crawl in beside her. With her comforting presence, I finally drifted off to sleep but woke the next morning feeling strange. I lay beside Mother and looked up over my head at the metal rungs of the bed frame against the wall. I felt hollow. I knew that life had changed forever, that things would never be the same. I could not put my feeling into words.

After breakfast Grandpa took Carol and me to the home of Mother's friends, Dan and Grace Suter, to spend the day. Not long before, our family had been there for a meal. Carol and I had played happily with toys that evening, and Mother thought it would be a good place for us to spend the day. A great deal would be going on at home with phone calls to make, neighbors stopping in with condolences and food, funeral and burial plans to arrange—more than enough without two little girls constantly underfoot.

Grandpa talked softly over my head, telling Dan and Grace the news they had not yet heard: Jacob Shenk, the president of the mission board and one of the most wealthy, influential men of the area, and my twenty-six-year-old father had both been killed in a plane crash in the mountains of eastern Tennessee. Jacob had been piloting his small Beechcraft Bonanza plane when they got into turbulent weather. Grandpa's words floated above me as I watched Mrs. Suter turn from the doorway and walk to the kitchen where she stood with her back to us. She is crying, I thought in the detached sort of way I would have noted that I had two hands. I didn't feel like crying. I didn't *feel*. It was as if I were looking in on an alien world from some, vast, impersonal distance—a world to which I had no connection. Yet somewhere in that vacant state, I wanted to be at home with Mother. I didn't want Grandpa to leave. I didn't want to be away from the small securities I still had. Mrs. Suter was OK. I trusted her, but she wasn't Mother. In the end, where I was didn't really matter because nothing mattered any more. I sat on the large living room rug and played with Carol as I was supposed to.

The events of the next days swirled around me and have drifted out of my memory, probably because there were too many to retain. Grandpa and Grandma Weaver came from Iowa, along with the Weaver aunts and uncles. Lehman relatives from Pennsylvania poured in. Grandpa's colleagues stopped by, as did neighbors and friends. Aunt Ada, my mother's aunt from next door, came one afternoon and quietly sat in a rocking chair next to Mother, who, in addition to grieving, still needed to rest from her surgery. Aunt Ada didn't talk. She just sat with Mother, a presence in her collapsed world. College students offered to help in any way they could. One young woman washed the kitchen floor on hands and knees, her tears adding to the wash water.

Left to right: **Carol, Mother holding Jeanie, and me—weeks after Papa's death.**

Where was I during those days? What did I do? Only one memory remains, a private moment that I kept to myself, not because it troubled me, but because it seemed so obviously true it merited no comment. Papa's casket stood in Grandpa's study, open some of the time for the visitors who stopped by. In one quiet moment when no one else was around, I stood silently and looked at my father's body in the open casket. In my three-year-old mind I had determined that the casket was not long enough to hold all of him. They must have cut his legs off at the knees to get him into such a short box, I thought in a matter-of-fact way. My family would have been consternated had they known what I was thinking and would have reassured me that his entire body was there, but I wasn't concerned. I assumed it must have been a necessary thing to do. After all, he was dead, and it didn't matter what anyone did to his body. What I knew was that my vibrant Papa was too big to fit into that box.

For a family prone to document everything with words, surprisingly little was written about those days. No one had the energy. We have only a picture taken a few weeks later. Mother sits in an easy chair in Grandma's living room holding tiny Jeanie. Mother has a wan smile on her lips. My parents' happy wedding picture, taken less than five years earlier, is displayed on the stand beside us. Carol is leaning against mother's right side. I am standing on her left, resting my arm on the arm of the chair but leaning on no one. Neither Carol nor I are smiling. Mother doesn't have her glasses on because she had been crying.

5

Life Goes On

I STOOD BESIDE MOTHER in the attic as she sorted through clothes stored in a box. Her slender hands lifted each garment in search of a particular item. "You need new shoes," she sighed, glancing at my scuffed brown tie shoes almost touching the box, "but I don't have the money." She paused. I looked down at my shoes. They did look scuffed and they pinched my toes. "I don't know what is going to happen to us," she sighed. I was puzzled. Why did she say that? I couldn't understand what the problem was.

"Grandpa will take care of us," I assured her. It worried me that Mother was worrying. Surely, she knew as well as I that Grandpa would never let us go without what we needed.

We now lived at Grandpa and Grandma's house. After the night Papa died, we never again slept in the apartment on the hill. Grandpa had decided within days of Papa's death to create an apartment for us on the second floor of their house, building two new rooms on the first floor to compensate for the loss of the upstairs rooms. Mother told me later that his decision was so quickly made that he asked out-of-town funeral guests to help move books off shelves to clear space for construction.

Naturally, I was not consulted about where we would live, but I surely would have said yes to living with Grandpa and Grandma. After our little house on Lost Creek, their house seemed spacious. Grandpa stood between us and the outside world; his physical presence alone assured me. He wasn't particularly tall, but he had broad shoulders, a square jaw, strong arms, and firm hands. His voice carried authority. Other people listened to him. When he talked to me his eyes crinkled into a smile. He never let me forget that I was his first, and therefore special, grandchild. I saw him as an endless source of whatever we needed. To me he was rich. I had no concept of how low faculty salaries were at the School.

Grandma thought they should have proceeded with more caution, giving Mother a chance to be part of the decision, but in Grandpa's great pain and shock, all he could think was to protect us. Mother's preference would have been to settle into an apartment of our own. She did not want to move back into her parents' home as a dependent after living on her own, but being numb and disoriented, she was not in a place to make a major decision. Besides, she had no financial resources and no viable alternative to suggest. We needed a place right away. Thus, it was decided with little deliberation—but with all the goodwill in the world—that we would live at Grandpa and Grandma's house.

Grandpa was not the only one who made me feel safe. Grandma brought a different kind of security. Grandpa went away every day to teach, while Grandma was always there—cooking, making a dress on her sewing machine, typing letters to family, doing laundry in the basement, hoeing in her garden. She braided my hair every morning after breakfast and told me endless stories. I followed her as she worked, and since she was an irrepressible teacher, she explained how she was doing each task. She always carried on conversations with me, almost as if I were an adult. She paid attention to what I said, engaged me, and never talked down to me.

In addition to Mother, Grandma, and Grandpa, the household offered my sisters and me a constant rotation of additional adult influences. Aunt Dot was still living with her parents. When I got up in the morning, I often went to the front porch, still in my nightgown, to meet her coming home from her night shift at the hospital. Even though I was getting big, she would pick me up and carry me into the house.

In the fall of our first year at Grandpa's house, she left to volunteer at a church-run hospital in Puerto Rico. We all went along to Richmond, where she boarded a train for Miami. I was sad at her going and stood on the station platform watching her wave to us as the train pulled out, surprised to see her wiping tears from her eyes with a white handkerchief. It puzzled me that she was crying. I could understand why *I* might cry at *her* leaving, but why was she? Adult tears troubled me. "Why is she crying when she is doing something she wants to do?" I asked. Grandma explained that sometimes, even when you were doing something you want to do, you could be sad, because you were leaving people you loved. Aunt Dot could be sad and happy at *the same time?* I thought about that for a long time. How could two such different feelings both be true?

Uncle Bob, who was in his last months of college, also lived at home. He was the youngest of Mother's siblings and her only brother. I trailed Uncle Bob endlessly, asking questions or just watching whatever he happened to be doing. He was Grandma's handyman, because Grandpa was usually too busy. "Uncle Bob, what are you doing?" I'd ask as he hammered or screwed some obscure pieces of wood together.

"Oh, something to make little girls ask questions," he would reply.

"No, what are you doing?" I would persist. Sometimes he made such a far-fetched explanation that I knew he was still teasing, but usually he explained the task at hand—except for one time. He built a little cupboard with double doors and two small drawers. It was just the right height for me. I was quite sure it must be for my sisters and me, but he wouldn't give the satisfaction of an answer until he finished it and painted it a light green. Finally, he admitted that it was for us. He took it up to our living room where we proudly placed our toy dishes and pans in it.

When he mowed the backyard with a push mower, I watched from a safe distance. I liked the whirring, rhythmic sound of the blades as he pushed and paused, pushed and paused, almost as if the mower needed to catch its breath between long pushes. I sometimes closed my eyes and breathed in the warm green smell of the cut grass. It filled me with a sense of well-being. It seemed that summer might last forever. When the mowing generated lots of clippings, Carol pulled me out of my intoxication by suggesting that we make a pretend house. We would rake the cut grass together with our fingers to create outlines of rooms for a playhouse where we pretended to live until Grandma raked it away.

I helped Uncle Bob water and feed chickens in the brooder house, even though the acrid smell burned my nose and made my eyes water. The chickens made more noise than a roomful of happy children, and the chicken house was hot under its tin roof. We walked along the metal troughs that ran the length of the room, pouring in feed. Then we filled the watering pans using a galvanized bucket with a spout. The chickens' jerky way of walking fascinated me. They always startled me by their rush to get water, even though I knew it was coming. Something about them felt untrustworthy. Their bright, darting eyes seemingly held no intelligence: they did not recognize me, even though I came often. I couldn't talk to them or make friends with them.

Left to right: **Uncle Bob, Aunt Esther, me (partially visible), and Aunt Dot holding Carol, who dearly wants a drink of whatever Uncle Bob has. I am quietly holding my own bottle out of Carol's line of vision.**

One of my favorite activities was to go with Uncle Bob to the ice house in town because I knew that meant we were going to make ice cream. The ice house seemed ancient. Years of use had smoothed the wooden floors to a silky patina under my bare feet. Cobwebs ridged with dust hung neglected in the corners. On a hot summer day, it was a cool place to be. I walked along the porch as we waited for our chunk of ice to be brought to us. The ice man put it in our brown burlap sack, and Uncle Bob swung it into the trunk of Grandpa's black Pontiac. Back at home Uncle Bob laid the sack on the backyard sidewalk, with the ice still inside it, and smashed it with the flat side of an ax. The bag kept the chips from scattering as he brought down the ax time after time. Meanwhile Grandma combined milk, sugar, eggs, and vanilla and poured the mixture into the ice cream freezer's metal canister, adding junket to make it clabber. When the ice was ready and the milk set, Uncle Bob stood the canister in the wooden freezer bucket. He poured ice from the sack all around it, adding salt between each layer of ice. Carol and I took turns sitting on the freezer while he turned the crank, presumably to weigh it down, but, given our skinny little bodies, it was mostly a way to let us participate. Sitting on the freezer with the ice crunching and slushing under me, and smelling the dusty burlap bag, I felt useful and brimmed with anticipation for the moment of tasting. When Uncle Bob finally pulled the paddle out of the stiff mixture, he sent us off to Grandma for a plate and *one* spoon. We always came back with enough spoons for us all.

Several times in the summer Uncle Bob mixed root beer and divided it into jars. We hovered like frustrated flies, following him to the hot back attic where he settled the jars carefully under the eaves so the fermentation process could begin. Later we helped him taste it to see if it was ready to put in the fridge. Homemade root beer was one of my favorite things to drink. If it had been up to me, we'd have drunk it quickly, but we could have only one glass a day. Sometimes it got old—too bitey and bitter for my honest preference. Uncle Bob still drank a glass of it. Carol and I said we liked it that way too. Maybe Carol did, but I only pretended. Grandma would tell Uncle Bob to throw out the rest. I hated to see it trickling down the drain. We should have been allowed to drink more of it.

Sometimes Uncle Bob brought home a girlfriend before or after some school function. If I was still up when they arrived, I tried to be as near to them as possible. One evening when they were sitting on the sofa, I managed to squeeze into the small space between them. I thought that this girlfriend was the prettiest, nicest person in the world. Then Grandma called me to help serve refreshments. Once I was in the kitchen, she quietly told me that I needed to let them sit next to each other and not bother them. I didn't see how sitting between them bothered them. They could still talk to each other. I served them Ritz crackers while Grandma poured grape juice, and then I reluctantly left them alone.

I was proud of Uncle Bob. He sang bass in a quartet called the Park View Melodians with three of his best friends. As far as I was concerned, they were famous. I knew they were often asked to sing for church services, revivals, and weddings. Sometimes right after church on Sunday they rushed off to sing on the local radio station, and Carol, Jeanie, and I huddled in front of Grandpa's radio to listen, with the adults not far behind us.

The Park View Melodians sometimes practiced at Grandpa's house, usually after we were in bed, but we could hear them singing and joking in the room below us. They often paused during their practice long enough to stand at the foot of the stairs to sing their fanciest song, "Kentucky Babe," for my sisters and me. "Bunka, bunka, bunka, bunka," they began in imitation of a banjo, and then the real words came in—"Skeeters are a hummin' in the honeysuckle vine / Sleep, Kentucky babe"—with the "bunkas" flowing up and down underneath the melody. I knew they were singing it for all of us, but I liked to think it was especially for me. Carol and Jeanie had been born in Harrisonburg, and I was the only one of us who had actually been born in Kentucky. These important men were singing for me.

During the first months we lived at Grandpa's house, Aunt Esther, Mother's next younger sister, was completing graduate school at Wheaton College near Chicago. Even though she wasn't around until summer, we knew her well. She had spent time with us in Kentucky and had been at Grandpa's on most of our previous visits. Grandma wrote to her every week, and once she told about Carol standing in the kitchen doorway and calling, "Aunt Esser! Aunt Esser!" repeatedly. Grandma commented that Carol was facing in the right direction (west), but she doubted that Carol's little voice carried all the way to Illinois. We were all extremely happy when Aunt Esther graduated and came home to begin teaching at the School.

Left to right: **Aunt Dot with me and Carol.**

6

Grandpa's House

GRANDPA'S BIG SQUARE STUCCO house embodied everything a square should. It was solid, balanced, predictable, and in right proportion. The cement footers were planted firmly on the limestone rocks and clay soil of Rockingham County, and its stucco walls reached to the tops of the big maples in the backyard. Positioned on the gentle slope of a hill, it rose to a four-story height above the street and provided exactly what I needed. Just walking up to it made me feel safe and a little bit important. The wide front porch with its wisteria vines that never blossomed provided privacy: I could look out at the world, unnoticed, from one of the wooden rocking chairs. I loved the glass knob on the front door and the carved wooden design below its window. The rooms of the house were much bigger than the rooms of any place I had ever lived. Light poured through the east windows, making the rooms alive—if, with nothing else, the continually drifting specks of dust caught in their beams. As I watched them, I wondered where the dust went when the light wasn't there.

The style of the house actually had a name: foursquare. It was hardly an imaginative one, but it described its structure accurately. It was one of thousands of foursquare houses built in the early decades of the 1900s: a cube with a hipped roof and dormers to the front and back and four nearly square rooms on each floor. I noticed many similar houses, but this one seemed unique and much more homelike than even its nearly identical partner next door, where Uncle Daniel and Aunt Ada lived. No house equaled Grandpa's.

The house smelled like home: apples or meat cooking on the stove, instant coffee, Ivory soap, the ink of new magazines, a hint of oily linoleum. It sounded like home, too. In the kitchen I heard water running and kettles clanking. There were busy sounds—the sharp clicking of typewriter keys and the more muffled up-and-down ticking of the sewing machine's needle. The screen door banged, the telephone rang, and there were voices—sometimes loud, other times quiet, but rarely angry. More often than not, music from Grandpa's Victrola or from the radio filled the rooms. Chapel services and choral programs from the School came through a loud speaker in the kitchen, sometimes almost drowned out by the hissing and whistling of the pressure cooker. On hot summer days the linoleum floors felt cool to my bare feet, and the living room, with its drawn shades, offered respite from the heat. In the winter it was warm, the hours punctuated with the banging of the furnace and the pinging or soft hissing of water in the radiators and pipes. Storm windows rattled when it was windy, and the floors and walls creaked.

Grandpa and Grandma Lehman as I first remember them,
standing in front of their house, ready to leave for a trip.

The house held more wonders than I could explore in a lifetime. To me, used to living on one floor, this house felt palatial—four levels, cases full of books and records, a piano, carpet on the living room floor and sheer window curtains, a rose-colored sofa with a graceful curved back and rolled arms. Grandpa's study had a big oak desk, which faced a wall of built-in oak bookshelves. The cellar held jars of canned food, and the freezer, as big as several bath tubs, seemed always full. The root cellar had the perpetual odor of dusty potatoes and overripe apples. In the attic stacks of old magazines lined wooden bookshelves, chests full of discarded clothes sat under the eaves, and a dormer window looked down over the street four stories below and all the way to Massanutten Peak on the horizon. Even though our apartment was on the second floor, we had freedom to go wherever we wanted.

Grandpa's house was equally Grandma's, and she clearly was the one who ran the day-to-day operations, but we always referred to it as Grandpa's house. We might have called it that for brevity's sake, but in reality, we referred to most families as if they belonged to the male—Chester's family, Daniel's family. Were we still Melvin's family? I thought so, but only people in Papa's family referred to us that way. Were we a real, legitimate family, or were we just a part of a family? Maybe that is why Grandpa was so important. He gave us legitimacy. We were Chester's grandchildren.

At home we were Miriam's family. Mother did her best to put her heart into fixing up our second-floor apartment. Grandpa and Grandma's front bedroom became our living room. It looked nothing like the proper downstairs living room, but it was the room in which we truly lived. A metal cot, or daybed, covered with a blanket became our sofa. Mother's dark blue padded rocking chair and a small footstool offered the only other adult seating. We had a child-sized metal folding table and two matching chairs. On the lower shelves of a ceiling-high bookshelf we kept our toys: blocks Papa had made for us, books, dolls, a toy car or two. Mother's books lined the upper shelves.

When Mother typed, she pulled her Royal typewriter on its wooden stand into the middle of the room. Papa had made the stand, so it was like having a little bit of him in the room. Her sewing machine stood at the south window, and the desk Papa built took up space on another wall. The room smelled faintly of the translucent, rose-strewn plastic curtains that hung at the sides of the windows, the windows themselves covered by sheers, with large fuzzy dots, like dotted Swiss on steroids. I thought the curtains were elegant. It didn't worry me that the floral wallpaper and "busy" linoleum on the floor, to say nothing of mismatched furniture, did not create a unified whole. Mother was there and that's what mattered.

A back bedroom became our kitchen, and everything there was new—sink, stove, refrigerator, table and chairs. I thought the gleaming white china closet was the best piece of furniture in the room. It had frosted flowers around the edges of the glass doors, and the backboard was painted bright red. In it, along with more mundane things, we kept our precious cereal box "Ranger Joe" mug and Mother's cream pitcher shaped like a cow, with a round open mouth from which to pour milk. Our new dinette set, positioned in front of double windows, looked out into the branches of the maple trees. Because of that, Mother named the room Maple Kitchen. A few years later she finished off the room with mint green wallpaper that had a diagonal lattice pattern with a cluster of deep red cherries in each diamond space. The red of the cherries matched the red in the cupboard. I loved everything about our fresh, new kitchen, but Grandma did not call it a bride's kitchen as she had when visiting Kentucky. Papa wasn't there.

Someone, meaning to be kind, gave Mother a whole case of canned peas. Compared to peas frozen fresh from the garden, canned ones tasted worse than flat, but Mother would not let any food go to waste. She created a winter Saturday night ritual: cream of pea soup. Using her vegetable ricer, she mashed a can or two of peas and made soup with them. Whatever it was that made the plain peas taste flat disappeared once they became soup—a miracle similar to water turning into wine as far as I was concerned. With a bit of bacon crumbled on top, the peas came to life again. To go with the soup, Mother cut slices of bright yellow Velveeta cheese, put them on soda crackers, and melted them under the broiler.

We often ate that meal by candlelight. I watched the flicker of the candles reflected in the big windows, and also the backward reflection of us eating out in the cold. There we looked drab and less substantial. I was glad to be inside where I could taste the warm salty soup and the melted cheese on crisp crackers, and where Mother's cheerful words reassured me, even though I knew she felt sad underneath. I would have liked to stay in that warm safety forever.

The second floor was never ours exclusively. That didn't occur to me as a problem, but from Mother's perspective the lack of privacy surely must have been less than ideal. Aunt Esther had the front corner bedroom opposite our living room, and the entire household shared the bathroom with its claw-foot tub, generous washbowl, and door to the balcony over the back porch.

The balcony was one of the wonders of the house. I could go out there and stand at the white painted railing to look down over the backyard and Aunt Ada's garden next door. Sometimes we played store on the balcony, transacting our business through an open kitchen window. We took turns buying and selling Jell-O, spices, and tin cans of soup or evaporated milk from the small metal cabinet that stood in the corner next to the window. At least once every summer we slept on the balcony, being sure to make our blanket beds between the ridged joints in the balcony's tin floor. After Queen Elizabeth's coronation it became the place where my royal personage waved graciously to the imagined adoring crowds cheering me from the backyard. Much less glamorously, it also served as a convenient place to shake out the dust cloth and the floor mop when I started cleaning Aunt Esther's room every Saturday.

I missed Papa. We talked about him frequently. Sometimes at breakfast Mother played a game with us, imagining Papa walking through the kitchen door and telling us what she thought he might say to each of us. That empty wooden doorframe stands clear in my memory. I looked at it so often—picturing him standing there, smiling at us—that it is almost as if he had been there in my memory. The reality of his absence remained the defining feature of life for me.

I sometimes talked with Grandma about my sadness, and one time she recorded what I said. I told her, "Mama and I just want our Papa, and we want him and want him and don't want nobody else but him." Another time, on a Sunday night when we three little girls had been fussy during church, Mother came home and cried. She had seen other women hand unhappy babies to their husbands and she felt particularly alone. After we had been put to bed, Grandma came into our room for some reason, and I said to her, "Grandma, do you remember that night when Papa died and Mama cried and Grandpa cried? Do you remember?"

"Yes, I remember," she replied.

"Well, that was such a sorryish time. I told Mama not to cry but she did. I don't like such sorryish times, do you?"

I was keenly aware of Mother's ache and sadness, even though she put on a cheerful front. Sometimes I could hear a strain that made her usually gentle voice sound forced and too bright. I could feel her ache around the edges of our Saturday evening meals. I knew her longing as she fixed up the kitchen to be a cheerful place. I felt her grief seeping out as she sat at her typewriter, typing a term paper for some college student in order to earn a bit of money, as she stood at the ironing board, ironing our dresses and hair ribbons, and when she turned to go alone to the living room after tucking us into bed. I couldn't lift her out of this no matter how many nice things I did for her.

No one ever told me that it was my job to keep Mother happy, probably because no one thought that. I didn't mention it either, because it was self-evident from my perspective. I learned to watch Mother closely, to judge every shade of change in her feelings, developing pitch-perfect mood detection where she was concerned. I could hear her forced cheerfulness and see her eyes sadden. I anticipated the things that would remind her of Papa and tried to match my affect to hers. I didn't want to fail her by being untouched by her sorrow. I was sad too. We were in this together in a way that didn't include my sisters. They were too little to understand. I kept trying to make her happy. She continued to grieve.

I lived in a strangely bifurcated world. I was safe and happy—life was as it should be. And at the same time, nothing was right. The worst had happened, and I had no power to keep it from happening again. I worried when Mother was late in coming home. Once when we visited in Kentucky several years after Papa's death, Mother went to an evening church service and left us with Mary, at whose house we were staying. I couldn't go to sleep and it seemed to me that hours and hours went by. I feared Mother would never return. I sat up and looked out the open window, feeling desperate, and praying out loud—begging would be a better word—that Mother would come back safely. I finally fell asleep. In the morning I was vastly relieved to see her, but that quickly turned to shame. At the breakfast table Mary laughingly told about checking on us and hearing my prayer. I felt embarrassed that my vulnerability had been observed and angry at the laughter. What was funny about me praying? And why was it silly for me to be worried about Mother's return? Clearly worry was something to hide, and prayers things to edit.

7

Paper Dolls

"Girls, come here! I have something to show you," Mother called. "I found my old catalog paper dolls." Hearing the excitement in her voice, Carol and I came running. "Remember how I told you we made paper dolls by cutting people and clothes from old Sears catalogs? Here they are!" Mother started taking pieces out of an old stationery box. "Here is the mother with a dress pinned on her. When I wanted the mother to wear another dress, I could unpin this one," she said, pulling out the straight pin, "and put on another. And here is the father." I watched eagerly as she took the rest of the family from the box—two boys, two girls, and a baby. She told us their names and sorted their clothing into stacks. Their suits, dresses, and coats looked old-fashioned and were much fancier than anything Mother or Grandma ever wore. Carol and I both wanted to play with them, so Mother began dividing them between us.

While I wanted to play with them, I didn't want her to separate them into two groups. I couldn't bear that thought. Here was a piece of her past that needed to stay intact. This family belonged together. To divide them was to violate something crucial—exactly what, I couldn't say, but I knew it was of ultimate importance. They needed to stay together as they were when Mother played with them. "No," I said, as Mother kept dividing them out, "No! Don't divide them."

"I thought you wanted to play with them," she said.

"But I don't want them divided."

"This will make it easier. You and Carol can each have some of your own," she said as she continued to make two stacks. "That way you won't argue." By this time, I was frantic. I began to cry. Mother's hand paused, then stopped, still holding a stack of paper clothes. I cried easily, so Mother didn't realize how strongly I felt in this moment. She tentatively laid out another dress and then a suit. I cried even harder, beginning to sob. Never had I felt such desperation, never such determination to keep something from happening. I cried hysterically. Nothing mattered to me now but keeping that paper doll family together.

"What is the matter?" she asked again. I was beyond answering. I couldn't stop crying. I could only sob. She stood quietly, looking at me. Then she carefully placed the paper dolls back in the box. Without a word she put on the lid and set it aside. Her silence worried me. Had I made her feel bad? She had been trying to do something nice for us and I stopped her. I couldn't understand why she hadn't seen the importance of keeping her family together. At least I had averted disaster. I felt relieved, but limp and exhausted. Mother went back to sorting through her trunk of old things, and I wandered away.

8

Park View

I stood at Mt. Clinton Pike, staring down the block to the end of the sidewalk. Just beyond its end stood a stubby tree whose trunk branched out to form a Y. The tree marked the southern limit of where I could go without permission. Beyond it lay vast space, flowing on forever—the rest of the world, as far as I was concerned. I would have called it infinity had I known the word.

As it was, I just stared at that Y in wordless fascination and longing. Was it the sense of an endless world beyond the sidewalk? Or did that dark Y amidst green leaves seem like an opening into another world, into other layers or realities? When I looked at the tree, it was easy to forget that ordinary houses lay beyond it. The Y felt mysterious and inviting, a doorway. Had I known about the back of the wardrobe leading into Narnia or platform nine and three-quarters at Kings Cross, from which the Hogwarts Express departed, I would have immediately recognized a similarity. I didn't really want to open that door. I didn't want the alluring distance to become just another ordinary part of my life. I preferred unimagined possibilities. I wanted the mystery to remain. I felt cautious about it too, not because I was afraid of the unknown, but because I was more comfortable with the familiar.

I often stood here, looking down the sidewalk to the Y. Behind me cars rushed by on Mt. Clinton Pike, and beside me Aunt Elizabeth's orange tiger lilies shifted in the breeze. They grounded me in time and place. I lived just three houses down the street.

Everything about this finite space was familiar: the scruffy lilies, the Wenger sisters' big brick house just across the street, other homes lining the street, and the things I couldn't see but knew were there—the tiny red spiders that ran along the gray limestone steps in front of Grandpa's house, the henhouse behind the grapevines, where I gingerly hunted eggs with Grandma, the well-worn path through Aunt Ada's garden that connected her house with ours, the hatchery where we went to see new chicks. I carried in my head every uneven section of the sidewalk where maple tree roots had heaved up the cement, making long roller-skating strides impossible. I knew Fellowship Hall, the big white building behind Phyllis's house where I sometimes went with Grandma on sewing circle days to watch her and other women sort through donated clothing or work on quilts or comforters. I knew the field across the street from us where Uncle Daniel kept his cow. I liked the stile at the back of the field, built just like the one pictured in our nursery rhyme book. Climbing it was my reward for having safely gotten past the cow who, in reality, paid little attention to my passing.

I had been in every house on the block, and I knew the names of almost everyone in each house. Most of them knew me by name, but for sure they knew I was Miriam's daughter, Chester and Myra's grand-daughter. They were kind to me, I imagined, because they knew my Papa had died.

The infinity beyond the Y wasn't completely unknown. Sometimes I walked into it with Grandma when we "went calling" on one of her friends. Once in a while I visited my friend Helen, who lived in a little square cinderblock house that smelled musty and felt cramped. Some-times Mother took me to play with Mary Jane while she and Mary Jane's mother visited, and on rare occasions we drove to the top of the hill where Papa's cousin and his family lived. From there we could look out over all the nighttime lights of Harrisonburg, twinkling like stars and stretching to the edges of my sight—one more alluring infinity of places where I didn't belong.

If I turned my back to the Y in the tree, I faced the other block of my world: the campus of Eastern Mennonite College. I never spent time gazing in that direction, maybe because it held no mysterious Y. The School offered certainty. Its schedule centered our everyday lives. Grandpa walked there every day to teach. Aunt Esther spent endless hours working in her classroom, and Mother studied there, to complete her bachelor's degree. Our days were bounded by morning chapel, which came through the loudspeaker connected to the sound system in the auditorium, by noon break, when Grandpa, Aunt Esther, and Mother came home for lunch, and by suppertime, which fell between the end of classes and any evening activities. Friday nights marked the time for literary society gatherings, which we attended with Mother. On Saturday evenings or Sunday afternoons, we often walked to the chapel for chorus programs. Life divided into fall and spring semesters and summer school. Spring was marked by homecoming and graduation, fall by the beginning of a new year and "School Day Out," an outing and picnic for the entire student body. Christmas was surrounded by numerous choral programs, a reading of Charles Dickens's *A Christmas Carol*, and the faculty performance of the cantata "Bethlehem" in the last chapel service before vacation began.

As on the block where I lived, there was no place on the campus unfamiliar to me. Its three main buildings, the "Ad Building" (Administration Building), the chapel, and the girls' dorm (North Lawn) had all been built by my Great-Uncle John Kurtz (distantly related to my future husband), and I knew them almost as well as my own house. The Ad Building in the center faced the eastern mountains, with the chapel to the south, and the girls' dorm to the north.

Sometimes in the summer, when Grandpa was away, I went "up to school" to get the mail. I liked this solo trip to the Ad Building where the mailboxes were. I counted slowly as I made my way up the many steps to its entrance, but I usually lost count after 20. The sun beat down on the unshaded, rough, cement stairs, and when I finally got to the top and entered the open double doors, the smooth tile floor felt cool under my bare feet. Even on warm days a breeze blew through the hall from the entrance doors at the back of the building to the ones in the front. It carried with it the smell of cleaning compound sprayed on mops used on the long hallway and of disinfectant from the bathrooms just inside the back entrance. Straight ahead hung a large clock, which ticked loudly, its sound reverberating from one end of the hall to the other. On the left, tucked under the staircase, was a little phone booth. Usually it was dark and deserted, but once in a while the light would be lit and someone would be sitting there, talking. I thought it would make a fun little playhouse. I stopped at the office next to it where Laura Histand, the receptionist and telephone operator, sat. I liked watching her push buttons when calls came in. Did she ever make a mistake and connect the wrong people? I wondered as I lingered, hoping she would offer me a piece of candy from the dish on her desk.

Next stop was the water fountain under the clock. Its ice-cold water hurt my teeth, and I had to stand on tiptoes to get a drink, but I always got one anyway. It was part of the ritual. Then I walked down the south hall to the mailboxes, which were next to the business office. I couldn't reach Grandpa's box, and even if I could have, I didn't know how to work the combination, so I had to ask at the business office window. Mr. Wise always noticed me standing there with my head just above the counter. He would come to ask how I was before getting the family's mail and handing it to me.

When I left the business office, I looked down to the library at the north end of the dim hall. I went there sometimes with Mother but never alone. I was intimidated by its tall bookcases holding mostly grownup books. I wouldn't have known how to find a book I'd like, even though I knew there were children's books there somewhere.

Then, with mail in hand, I went back down the long flight of steps and walked along College Avenue, past the chapel again, to Mt. Clinton Pike. There I paused to look carefully both ways before crossing. Once across, I paused again to see the Y in the tree before I proceeded down the street and ran up the steps to Grandpa's house, glad to be home again.

The chapel was as familiar as the Ad Building. I knew well the long, uncushioned wooden benches that smelled of varnish and got tacky in hot weather, causing my dress or bare legs to stick to the seat. Huge arch-topped windows rumbled when ushers opened them with long wooden poles. Big box speakers hung from the ceiling, each with an opening into its dark interior. For some reason, my sisters and I pretended that lions lived in them. It was a safe kind of scariness because we knew it wasn't true.

The cool chapel basement housed Aunt Esther's combo classroom and office. I sometimes went there to look at pictures in her sets of reading books or to watch her working at her collection of homemade, teaching aids—pictures from magazines, construction paper squares and circles cut in parts to illustrate fractions, hand-printed charts. She had an abacus that I liked to play with and a large paper cutter worthy of the name "guillotine." I didn't need to be told not to touch it.

Across the hall from her room was another classroom where children's meetings were held on Sunday or Wednesday evenings during adult services upstairs. That room was dominated by a large oil painting of Dirk Willems pulling his pursuer out of the broken ice of a river. Grandma helped me look up the original picture in the *Martyrs Mirror,* a thick book that told about early Anabaptist martyrs. She told me the story of this man who was arrested because of his beliefs in God. He was running away from a would-be captor but turned back to rescue his pursuer who broke through the ice while chasing Dirk across a frozen river. The rescued man wanted to let Dirk go free, but other authorities arrested him anyway and executed him. This was a different kind of scary than the lion boxes upstairs. I studied the picture carefully every time I sat in that room and wondered if I could ever be that brave.

The chapel basement also housed the assembly room where literary society meetings took place, where the Ladies' Chorus processed in, holding candles, and singing "Brightest and Best" at the beginning of their Christmas program, and where "Brother" Brackbill, one of the faculty members, recited Dickens's *A Christmas Carol*.

The girls' dorm was the newest of the three buildings, not yet completed. Once in a while we visited someone in one of the rooms, which smelled of new plaster and had cold, uninviting tile floors. Grandma's friend Miss Kemrer, who taught Latin and Greek, had a small apartment in the front corner of the first floor, and the school's dining room was in the basement. The back staircase smelled smoky from the incinerator at the bottom of the stairwell.

If the School was the beating heart at the center of my world, Park View was the body around it. Park View began as a string of houses along Mt. Clinton Pike (now part of Chicago Avenue) called "String Town." As Eastern Mennonite School grew, the village spread out around the campus, and, as the School expanded into a college, Park View expanded along with it. Nearly all of our neighbors had moved here because of the School. They were teachers, administrators, or students.

Park View felt like an extension of Grandpa's house—not a square, but solid, predictable, and inhabited by adults who were present to me. It offered familiarity and safety.

I sometimes sat on Grandpa's granite front steps, warmed from the sun, and watched my world go by. Jacob Martin, walking home from his store, always tipped his hat to me, and Robert Messner, one of the chicken hatchery workers, did the same. The Shenk girls, who had lost their father in the plane crash along with Papa, lived next door to the hatchery. Ellen walked by to school every day, and sometimes Virginia Ann clopped by on her horse. Between our house and the Shenks' lived the Brunks.

Gerald, George, and Paul had more important things on their minds than a little neighbor girl as they biked past, but Conrad at least teased me, and I played with their sister, Barbara. The five Mumaw sisters, who lived at the end of the sidewalk, went by every day on their way to and from the School. They usually smiled and said hi. Once I tried to sell one of them a small bouquet of flowering weeds picked from the lawn and stuffed into a small frozen orange juice can. She declined, and I felt disappointed. John Mumaw, their father, who was president of the college, greeted me by name when he went by. Once on a School Day Out he noticed students clustering around my mother and my cute little sisters while I stood on the sideline. He squatted down to my level and conversed with me. It felt good to be noticed by a grown-up.

My sisters and I moved as easily along College Avenue as we did between the upstairs and downstairs of Grandpa's house. We walked over to Shenk's Hatchery to watch the men working there. They greeted us by name and let us watch them vaccinate chicks, sticking a hand into a flat of fuzzy yellow peeping chicks, lifting one out and injecting it close to its beak. Some days I was brave enough to hold a wiggling little chick. It filled and warmed my hand, but I held it carefully so it couldn't peck me. I puzzled over the way such a fluffy cute handful could turn into a big, scary chicken.

I liked to go next door to play with Barbara. Sometimes we paused in the house to watch her mother ironing her husband's white shirts on her big mangle. We didn't have one, and the way the two big rollers came together, pressing long pieces of shirt or sheet fascinated me. It was much faster than Grandma's iron but much bulkier. In the backyard Barbara and I watched as Conrad and Paul played with a large blanket tent they had erected, a replica of the real one their father used for his revival meetings. Their toy tractor trailers even had the same campaign logo on their sides as the real trucks: "The Whole Gospel for the Whole World." I thought it would be fun to play with them, but Barbara and I were too young and besides, we were girls. Revival tents and trailer trucks were for boys.

Sometimes Mother or Grandma sent me to the College Shop to buy a box of cereal or crackers. I could walk there, cutting through the Wenger sisters' big yard so as not to walk on the edge of Mt. Clinton Pike. The little white stucco shop, which stood just beyond Martin's Store, catered primarily to students and faculty, serving coffee, donuts, ice cream, and other snacks along with a few groceries. On lucky days, when Lois, one of the Mumaw sisters, was working there, she sometimes dipped me a vanilla or strawberry ice cream cone from one of the big gallon containers in the glass-topped freezer case. On those occasions I walked home slowly, licking my cone, balancing the desire to make it last as long as possible with the need to finish it before my sisters saw it.

Other times Grandma sent me to Dwight's Grocery Store on the edge of Park View. To get there, I crossed the street right in front of Grandpa's house, walked through Uncle Daniel's cow pasture, through his son Harold's yard—where we sometimes went to play with Kenny and Danny—and across another street to the store. Even there I felt safe. If I got confused with nickels and dimes and calculating what I needed to pay, I simply opened the coin purse and dumped its contents on the counter, so Dwight could help me count out the right change. I trusted him with money, but I didn't expect him to offer me a treat. He wasn't a part of my Mennonite world.

There were places in Park View I didn't go alone but often went with an adult. I walked with Grandma to get tomato plants, onion starts, and petunia seedlings at Brunk's greenhouse just across Mt. Clinton Pike, in the same block as the chapel. When we stepped into the humid, earthy-smelling greenhouse I felt like I was in a different world. Water dripped somewhere, and everything was damp and covered with green moss. I was not sure I liked the almost muddy paths between wooden raised beds of plants, but I loved the musty smell. Grandma and Mrs. Brunk visited while Grandma made her choices and paid for them. I helped carry things home. Sometimes, if we were getting a lot, we brought along our red wagon.

A new dress meant going to Martin's store to choose fabric and perhaps a pattern. This store was a place of many wonders besides fabric. They sold shoes, sweaters, underwear, hosiery, socks, and every imaginable kind of handkerchief arranged in a large drawer in the front corner of the store. They also sold coverings for women, each size and style in a separate compartment in a drawer next to the hankies. Above the drawers was a large mirror where women could check out the appearance and fit of a covering. I didn't yet need a covering, but I liked to stand and look at myself in the mirror when I got bored waiting for Mother to decide what she wanted.

Jacob Martin sometimes let us choose shoes without charging us, as a way of helping Mother. She appreciated his kind gesture but felt awkward accepting "charity." The choices were limited so we couldn't always get exactly what we wanted. I wasn't excited about the brown tie school shoes Mother chose for me, but I wore with pride the mirror-shiny, black patent leather Mary Janes she got me for Sunday.

We went to town only when we needed something that couldn't be bought in Park View. Harrisonburg never felt as comfortable to me. It was part of a larger, stranger world where we didn't quite belong. All I had to do was notice how differently we were dressed to know that. Other girls my age had short hair, not pigtails. They didn't wear long brown stockings in the winter, and their mothers didn't have cape dresses or bonnets. Mother always wore her bonnet to town, and that in itself was a sign that town was foreign. Women of my mother's generation wore bonnets mostly when they went outside a Mennonite community.

Overt violence or crime was unknown to me. We never locked doors, either house or car, even when we went on trips. A casualty that did occur was a mother possum and her babies found dead on the street in front of our house. Grandma called Carol, Jeanie, and me to come see them early one summer morning. I stood and studied the little lima-bean sized babies scattered all over the blacktop like little pink commas. Grandma told us not to pick them up. After we had examined them, Grandpa came with a shovel and buried them, along with their mama, in the garden.

Only once did we see a policeman on our street. That was the night Mr. Hopkins came to Grandpa's house. He and his family sometimes attended our church. Grandpa, who was the pastor, and Mr. Seitz would visit him, trying to persuade him to stop drinking. We all knew that drinking was sinful, and we prayed for him to become a Christian and stop drinking. Even though I knew that he was a "drunkard" and had overheard snatches of adult conversation about the problems his family dealt with, I had never seen him like this.

He stumbled up the steps to the house and knocked on the door. I peered around Grandma and Aunt Esther, watching from the safety of the kitchen hallway as he spoke to Grandpa with slurred, almost incoherent, speech. What we could understand made little sense. After trying unsuccessfully to talk with him, Grandpa took Mr. Hopkins's arm in his strong grip and led him back down all the steps to his car. Maybe Grandpa took his keys. It was clear Mr. Hopkins was in no shape to drive. Grandpa came back inside, and I watched as he got out the phone book, found the number for the police, and dialed decisively. He gave our address, but nothing else seemed familiar. Grandpa was calling some uniformed person from outside our world for help rather than asking a neighbor, as he usually would have done. Mr. Hopkins brought drama beyond our usual quiet evenings, and now the police were coming.

We watched from the window of the study as the police car pulled up to Mr. Hopkins's car and parked under the streetlight. Two policemen got out, helped him into the back of their car, and drove off into the dark, taking him to town where he would spend the night in jail.

I worried that it might not be Christian to let the police take him rather than fixing a place for him to spend the night with us. Weren't we to befriend anyone who came to the door? Why did we make exceptions? Were we not willing to be inconvenienced by a man who tottered and made no sense? I couldn't puzzle out Grandpa and Grandma's response. If it had been someone like us, Grandma would already be making up a bed for the person. Why would they rid themselves of this responsibility and let Mr. Hopkins go to jail—a fate worse than death in my mind? I didn't question them. I trusted that they were doing the right thing, but I just couldn't understand it.

Me sitting on the limestone steps where little red spiders crawled.

Park View was not idyllic. The daddy of one of my friends would get angry and yell at his children. Once he cut up a pair of high-heeled dress-up shoes my friend and I argued over. Even though they were not my shoes, I was dismayed by the destruction. It seemed a waste to cut up the shoes rather than help us figure out how to share, as Mother or Grandma would have done. And I felt something new. The stark sight of these favorite dress-up shoes, cut through the middle with all the internal layers showing, made me feel cut in half too. A good thing had been violated, destroyed. Something about that felt dangerous. I had no idea how to talk about it, so I tried to avoid going there when he was home.

9

Hair Combing

EVERY MORNING GRANDMA COMBED my hair. Mother combed Carol's tangled curls upstairs, accompanied by Carol's wails and screams of protest, but I went downstairs to the peace and quiet of Grandma's kitchen. I seated myself on her tall kitchen stool next to the washbowl and waited. Grandma was usually washing her breakfast dishes, but she stopped when I arrived and came, drying her hands on her apron.

She always started with my right braid, unbraiding it all the way up to the top. Then, dampening the brush under the washbowl spigot, she began to brush through my thick hair. When she came to a "snarl" she reached for the comb and carefully, starting at the bottom, used the end tooth of the comb to work it out. "Never start at the top," she told me. "That just makes the snarl worse. Start at the bottom and pick out a little bit at a time."

When Grandma was satisfied that my hair was thoroughly brushed, she began the intricate French braiding process, starting with small strands of hair just above my forehead, braiding them, and gathering in more hair with each new interweaving until she had all the hair incorporated into a braid that reached halfway down my back. She fastened it with a rubber band. Then she began the other side. Every so often she would use her fist to push gently in the middle of my back, saying "Sit up straight." I would straighten up for a little while but then forget and slump again, causing her to remind me once more.

As she braided, she told me stories from her childhood—stories about sticky tobacco worms she and her sisters had to pick off plants in the hot sun, the spring house that was cool even on the hottest summer days, the excitement of finding an orange beside her plate on Christmas morning, the playhouse her father made for her and her sisters above the carriage house, and the cracked and nicked dishes her mother gave them to furnish it. She told me about the first time she saw her mother cry, when her cousin died of lockjaw (tetanus) after falling out of a tree. There was the story of the time her father reported to her mother that Myra (Grandma) had thrown two small stones at him, and she, little-girl Myra, hearing his report had declared, "I frowed free." She remembered how her father had laughed at that, shaking his head in amusement. "She frowed free," he said over and over as he chuckled to himself.

I liked hearing about her and Grandpa's move from Lancaster County to Virginia and into Cinder Path Cottage, a little house in the middle of a cornfield, named so by Grandpa because of the path to it he created with cinders. She described how she enjoyed dressing up my mother for church when she was a baby and how Mother, when she was a bit older, complained at nap time because she wouldn't get her playing done.

I especially enjoyed hearing about the day I was born and how excited she and Grandpa were to get the phone call from Papa. She told about visiting us in Kentucky and riding a horse across a stream while everyone else turned to watch, laughing. They told her, once she was safely across, that the week before, the horse she was riding had decided to lie down in the stream, giving its rider a dip in the water.

Some days, as she began brushing out my hair, she recited poems along with commentary about their meaning or background history. She had a large store from which to draw, primarily from nineteenth-century New England poets: Henry Longfellow, Ralph Waldo Emerson, John Greenleaf Whittier, and James Russell Lowell. I took for granted her faultless memory. Words flowed out, sometimes in gushing rivers and other times in slow, deliberate streams, words singly or grouped together, always with her clear, crisp diction.

Poems were as good as stories; they were stories, just with better words. In "The Children's Hour," by Longfellow, I imagined my sisters and me as "Grave Alice, and laughing Allegra, / and Edith with golden hair," running down to their father's study, just as we did to Grandpa's. Paul Revere's gaze at the "belfry-tower of the Old North Church" and his advance from village to village held even more drama than any of Grandma's childhood stories. And I could almost taste the dust made by the advance of Confederate soldiers up the streets of Fredrick, Maryland, toward the Union flag flapping bravely in the wind in Whittier's "Barbara

Frietchie." I repeated the opening lines over and over to myself, relishing the smooth flow of words and the pictures they created:

Up from the meadows rich with corn,
clear in the cool September morn,
The clustered spires of Fredrick stand
Green-walled by the hills of Maryland.

Sometimes I didn't know the meaning of words. "*Ermine* too dear for an earl" and "sheds new-roofed with *Carrara*" sounded beautiful no matter what those strange words meant.

Some poems she recited were less poetic, but fun.

Away, away in the Northland,
Where the hours of day are few,
And the nights are so long in winter
That they cannot sleep them through.

This Phoebe Cary poem tells of an old woman who baked successively smaller cakes for Saint Peter but considered each of them too large to give him. Finally, in a fit of anger, Saint Peter turned her into a woodpecker.

Once in a while Grandma would quote James Whitcomb Riley's "Little Orphant Annie" with its refrain:

An' the Gobble-uns 'at gits you
  Ef you
    Don't
      Watch
        Out!

My sisters and I quoted that line to each other even though we knew goblins were made up. It was easy to laugh in the daylight, but I checked under my bed each night. It seemed a little less funny then.

When my hair was neatly braided, the stories or poems came to an end. Grandma looked with satisfaction at my two neatly braided pigtails. She had done her part to ensure that her granddaughter did not have "strubbly" hair. That was as important as standing up straight and enunciating words clearly.

10

Stories

"NINE O'CLOCK AND ALL'S well. Nine o'clock of a rainy night." Carol and I lay in bed together in our attic bedroom, and I imagined a town crier on the street below. If I closed my eyes, I could see him clearly: lantern in one hand, ladder for lighting streetlights in the other, rain dripping off his hat, his shoes striking the wet brick pavement—just like the picture in Marguerite de Angeli's *Thee Hannah*! He wasn't real, of course. We were in Park View, where the streetlights came on automatically at dusk, prosaic cement sidewalks lined only one side of the street, and we told time by a white electric clock on the kitchen wall. No need for a town crier or lamplighter. What was real, though, was the rain gently falling on the tin roof above us. We snuggled under the covers and continued imagining a world far removed from our own.

Our pretend stories in bed were often the continuation of what Mother had just read to us. She loved reading, and we loved listening in equal measure. After we got into our nightgowns, she would settle into her rocking chair in our upstairs living room and open a book. As she began to read in her pleasant, melodic voice, my eyes would wander to her smooth forehead edged by black hair. She combed it straight back with a part not quite in the middle because of a slight widow's peak. Her mouth opened and closed as if it were a function that went on, free of any effort on her part. I became mesmerized as I watched her. But I listened to the story as well and became part of a different world. I lay in bed with Laura and Mary in their snug cabin in the big woods of Wisconsin, watching the fire crackle while Pa sang them to sleep, accompanied by his fiddle. I picked blueberries with Sal on a Maine hillside, hearing each berry plunk into my bucket, and I watched Johnnie's bear grow from a cub to a giant who wreaked havoc wherever he went.

One book, *Henry's Red Sea,* belonged in a category unlike any other—not that it was better written or more exciting, although it contained excitement. It told the story of a Russian Mennonite family displaced by WWII and aided by Peter and Elfreda Dyck to escape from East Germany. The cozy picture I conjured up surely didn't match the reality of a drafty Berlin shelter where each family strung sheets for privacy. I felt great satisfaction in the surprising appearance of Henry's missing father at the end of the story. But even that failed to catapult the book into its special category. It's what happened next. Mother closed the book when she finished reading and said rather casually, "I know Peter Dyck." I stared at her, astonished. "What?" I said. "You know Peter Dyck!" I knew some stories were true, but it had never occurred to me that someone as ordinary as Mother would know a person famous enough to be written about in a book. To be part of a story printed in a book meant that one was famous, but my world didn't include famous people. Mennonites weren't famous because being famous meant living in the world outside of ours. Mother knowing Peter Dyck brought me as close as I could hope to touching fame.

Bible stories inhabited a category all their own. Mother read them to us in the morning for family worship, usually just after breakfast. She had a big, brown Bible storybook by Elsie Egermeier. I listened to the stories, hearing them all as literal accounts of long-ago events. Old Testament stories were filled with drama and unexpected happenings. My sisters and I pored over the pictures of Elijah being carried off in a fiery chariot and of King Nebuchadnezzar with talon-like fingernails, eating grass. I wondered how it would feel to live like a wild animal as he did. What went on inside his head? Did he wish to be human again or did he think like an animal?

My favorite story, though, was about the little room a woman fixed up for the prophet Elisha. Our book had no picture with this story, but I didn't need one. I imagined an inviting space with a lighted lamp on a worn wooden table. Rich-colored blankets covered a single bed, and earth-colored walls added to the warm glow. I would have liked such a room for myself.

Stories of Jesus teaching and his disciples fishing paled in comparison. They sounded more everyday: men walking on dusty paths, people arguing with Jesus or listening to him talk, Paul traveling—also on long, dusty roads—or getting thrown into prison. True, people were healed, but that was part of the taken-for-granted goodness of Jesus. Of course Jesus healed people. Of course crowds followed him. Of course he could walk on water, or still the sea, or feed thousands of people with five loaves and two fish. Of course he died and rose again. Of course he loved me. He was perfect and perfection didn't invite much imagination.

I took for granted that God was all-powerful, that God was perfect, that God loved me and wanted me to be good, that God punished people who didn't obey him, that Papa went to be with Jesus in heaven, and that we would see Papa when Jesus came again.

It was wrong to question anything about the Bible, but I was aware of a discrepancy between what I had been taught and my own experience. God wanted me to be good, which meant listening to Mother, not getting into arguments with my sisters, not lying. I also knew that God was all-powerful, which meant that God could do anything he wanted. (God was always *he* in those days.) If God had all that power, why didn't he make me be good? I felt a little guilty saying it, but it must be his fault that I wasn't. Yet I couldn't blame God because God was perfect. I couldn't work out this seeming contradiction. Maybe I could when I was older.

11

Playtime

GRANDPA'S STRONG HAND GRASPED the hammer, and his sun-browned arm swung with focused efficiency. The force of his swing and the ring of hammer meeting nail with exact precision held me spellbound. I couldn't leave. The power of his blows made me want to hold my breath. I moved back a little, trying not to imagine a finger or bare toe in the way of that forceful tool. I also tried not to think of this same arm swinging an axe down on the neck of a frightened chicken, whose headless body then flopped around in a most alarming way. Safety and danger were tied up together in the strength of his arms. I wasn't afraid—I was never afraid of him—but, just the same, I kept a safe distance from his hammer.

Grandpa did nothing by half measures. He approached each task as the worthiest, most important endeavor of the moment. Right now, it was pounding nails. He knelt on the part of the floor that was finished and added one new board and then another. He was making a new floor for a playhouse under the front porch, where, many years ago, he had dug out space for his own daughters. I could easily stand up straight in it, but he had to stoop or kneel.

I liked being with Grandpa. I was confident that he would never let anything hurt me. I was also confident that he loved me. Whenever I wandered into his study, no matter how busy he was, he always looked up and smiled and pointed to the picture of him holding me, mounted in his round glass paperweight. He would ask, in a puzzled tone, "Who *is* that little girl?" This was one of our rituals, along with his telling me every afternoon, as he sat at the kitchen table with his cup of instant Nescafe coffee, that he liked a little cream in his "Caffy," blending Kathie and coffee into a single word. I usually wandered off after our little jokes because what Grandpa was doing held little interest for me.

Watching him work on the playhouse was an entirely different matter. This interested me. In the late afternoon heat, sweat ran down his temples. He paused to pull a big white hankie out of his hip pocket and wipe his face. He smiled at me, the lines around his lively eyes crinkling. He made a small joke, not so much funny as affectionate, reassuring me that he was aware of me standing there, barefooted, in a cotton summer dress.

It took several days for the floor to be completed because Grandpa worked at it only in the late afternoon, when he had finished his school work. I waited impatiently, eager for him to be finished. Finally, he was, but he had one more task—building a shelf along the bottom of the screen frame that filled the space from the porch floor to the yard outside. This would be the counter where I could stand, looking out through the screen as I prepared pretend meals. I was eager to bring in my little plastic set of orange and blue canisters, bowls, and the amazing little stand mixer that had beaters that actually rotated when I turned the crank.

Once Grandpa's part was finished, he went back to his usual outside work of tilling the garden. Now it was Mother's turn to help us fix up the playhouse. Although she was much smaller than Grandpa, she too had to stoop or kneel in order not to bump her head on the porch floor joists. Her presence was different from Grandpa's. It felt calm, quiet, and sooth-ing in contrast to the noisy pounding and the bigger-than-life enthusi-asm Grandpa exuded. She spoke in a lilting voice about what we could do to make the playhouse pretty and cozy. She brought down the green cupboard Uncle Bob had made for us and carried in the little table that Grandpa built for her and her sisters when they were little. I helped hang printed feed sack curtains over the side screens and watched her place an old rag rug on the floor, making the space softer and homier.

"Now I think your house looks cozy and ready to use," she said as she flattened out a wrinkle in the rug. "Would you girls like to eat break-fast here tomorrow morning?"

"Yes, yes," I said, clasping my hands together. I hadn't even imagined something as wonderful as this.

I woke early the next morning and rushed downstairs from our attic bedroom to stand at her door. "Mother," I said. "Are you awake?"

She half opened her eyes and mumbled, "Why are you up so early?"

"I'm ready for breakfast," I said. "Get up!"

"It's too early. Go do something in the living room for a while." I wandered slowly to the living room and found a book to look at, but I wasn't interested. In a short time, I was back at her door.

"Mother, wake up!" I demanded.

She sighed, closing her eyes for a moment, and then threw back the covers. "OK. I might as well get up."

I hurried off to wake Carol and Jeanie. By the time we came back to the kitchen Mother had filled the cow pitcher with milk. She put cereal in our bowls and poured small glasses of orange juice. We trailed behind her as she carried the food to the playhouse on the wooden tray Papa had made. She placed our bowls and juice glasses on the little table and left. I dipped my spoon into my cereal, eager to eat before it became soggy. Corn flakes had never tasted this uncommonly good, nor had juice been so sweet. I didn't notice the slightly bitter after-taste that made me not sure I liked orange juice. Everything seemed as fresh and new as the morning, as fresh and new as our playhouse, which still held the echo of Grandpa's pounding and the warm comfort of Mother's touch.

When I finished my cereal, I stood at the little counter looking out at the sun, newly risen over the blue Massanutten Peak. A million drops of dew sparkled on the nearly eye-level grass in the yard. Birds sang. Joy filled my chest, radiating down to my toes, still wet from the morning dew, out to the tips of my fingers, and up to the top of my yet uncombed hair. I was flooded with a sense of complete well-being. I felt a flash of sparkling clarity in which the day, the summer, and life itself stretched out invitingly. Anything was possible. Everything alive.

Carol and I paused on the curb and looked carefully in each direction. Grandma stood behind us watching, but she did not follow us across the street. Sometimes we accompanied her when she called on Mrs. Shupp, but today was different. Carol and I had been invited there for tea, just the two of us. Mrs. Shupp was as old as Grandma and lived across the street from Uncle Daniel and Aunt Ada in a big stone house. She had the whitest hair I had ever seen, "exactly like her father, old Anthony Heatwole," Grandma said.

We had changed out of everyday dresses to nicer ones, and our hair was freshly combed, so we would look "presentable." We were too old to hold hands for crossing the street, yet Carol stayed close beside me. I felt a little nervous as I, being older, knocked at Mrs. Shupp's door. Her warm welcome melted my anxiety. She led us into her dining room, and there before us lay a sight straight out of a storybook. The room was dim and cool and felt like a world apart from the bright sunny day outside. Lace curtains, much fancier than Grandma's plain ones, covered the windows. A china closet stood along the wall, full of pretty dishes. Grandma's dishes were all on ordinary cupboard shelves behind wooden doors, but Mrs. Shupp's were on display—every teacup and saucer and flowered serving bowl, every glass jelly dish and salt cellar. The table was set unlike any I had ever seen. It was covered with a white lace tablecloth, and a bouquet of pink and purple larkspur from her garden stood in the center. What my eyes focused on, though, was a glistening white cake on a glass, pedestaled cake server, its white frosting sprinkled generously with coconut. I had never seen anything so elegant in my life. Just seeing it would almost have been enough. My eyes moved on to three places set with china tea cups and small plates, much more delicate than any we had at home. The cloth napkins were edged with lace.

We sat down, almost wordless with awe. "Now you girls wait," Mrs. Shupp said, "while I get the tea." She disappeared into the kitchen and returned in a moment with a pot of tea. She poured some into each of our cups and offered us sugar from her cut glass bowl. I carefully stirred in a spoonful and then added milk from a matching glass cream pitcher, not wanting to miss out on any part of this. I felt grown-up as I sat stirring the way I had seen Grandma do, enjoying the ring of my spoon against the thin side of the cup and watching the steam rise and swirl. Before she sat down, Mrs. Shupp asked us each if we would like a piece of coconut cake—as if that were in question. She cut generous slices, not skinny little girl pieces adults sometimes offered us. I had never had a coconut cake before, but I was sure I could eat a whole piece no matter the size.

At our house, layer cakes were reserved for birthdays or School Day Out, when each of the faculty women baked a layer cake for the students. And we never sat down for tea and cake in the middle of the afternoon. I ate slowly to make those moments last as long as possible. I wanted to live like this, I thought to myself—to have tea and cake in the afternoon, to have dishes this pretty and a table looking this elegant.

Mrs. Shupp chatted away, having no idea that she had just raised the bar for beauty and style in my life. From now on I would try to imagine how I could set a table as pretty as hers. I would dream of baking a cake that looked as pristine as this coconut confection. I would wish for dainty pink and purple flowers like those from her garden, rather than our garish orange marigolds with their pungent smell, which added color but no style to a table.

When our cake and tea were finished, we sat at the table talking. I wanted to prolong the party as long as I could, but Mrs. Shupp looked at her watch and said it was four o'clock, the time Grandma said we should come home. Carol and I reluctantly got up from the table. I hope I thanked her as I had been instructed to do. We said goodbye and carefully crossed the street. Then, leaving behind any pretense of dignity, we ran up the front steps as fast as we could, eager to tell everyone about the glorious party.

As vitally alive as our real world was, we created more places to inhabit. Jeanie was enough younger that she often wasn't a part of Carol's and my pretending. Our first imaginings were ordinary, modeled on people we knew. We played "John and Marjory Burkholder," neighbors around the corner. John sold Grandpa his Pontiacs, which elevated him to celebrity status in Carol's eyes, but they shopped in the same stores we did and attended the same music programs at the School. Our play centered on familiar activities.

As our worlds expanded, we began to envision new possibilities beyond our everyday lives. When King George VI of England died, we heard about it in the news. I stood beside Mother at her sewing machine in our living room, looking out at the leafless black branches of a maple tree on a rainy, winter day and talked with her about the grieving queen. I spent time looking at pictures of the king's funeral in *Life* magazine. I could not yet read, but I studied people's faces and postures. The pictures told me all I wanted to know, especially one of the three queens—Elizabeth, her mother, and her grandmother—all veiled and standing together watching the approach of the king's coffin. I returned to that picture again and again because I recognized their feelings. Even though our circumstances were different, I felt connected to Elizabeth, the new queen. She, like I, had no father.

A few months later, in the summer before Elizabeth's coronation, Grandpa and Grandma made a trip to attend the Mennonite World Conference in Switzerland, the trip of a lifetime for both of them. (Grandma's way was paid by Grandpa's congregation—otherwise she wouldn't have been able to go along.) In addition to the conference, they toured places in the Middle East and Europe, including Buckingham Palace and Westminster Abbey in London. Although it was still a year away, London was already preparing for the coronation. Grandma brought home a picture book for me titled *Our Young Queen*. It became my most prized possession, and I spent hours looking at the pictures. I thought Elizabeth was beautiful. Everything she wore fascinated me—open-toed high heels, broad-brimmed hats, a fur wrap, elegant gowns, necklaces, and earrings. I tried to fashion my own versions of those things—earrings made from fancy buttons attached to blasting wire I had collected after roadwork on our street, wraps made of old curtains or scarves, hats out of anything that could be pressed into service. I would stand in the attic looking at myself in an old mirror, imagining a fine hall behind me rather than open rafters and stacks of old magazines.

I was ready when Elizabeth's coronation day finally came. That morning Grandpa came up to my attic bedroom before six o'clock, wrapped me in a quilt, and carried me downstairs to sit with Grandma in front of the radio. We didn't have a television, but we had a double-spread picture from *Life* magazine showing the interior of Westminster Abbey and a numbered sequence of where each part of the ceremony would take place. As it progressed, Grandma helped me follow the numbered picture and explained what was happening. I sat engrossed for the whole service. It seemed so vibrant and full of pageantry that my own life felt strange. I wasn't sure I wanted to reenter the familiar reality of the study, with its tan linoleum and green window shades, while something else glistened so enticingly in that far-off place. I waited eagerly for the next *Life* magazine and the pictures it would surely have. They would carry me back to that enthralling experience. I adored Elizabeth—she was my star, my hero.

From this beginning, Carol and I created a country we called Gugog. I can't say for sure where Carol's ideas came from, but I know mine were a blend of British royalty and the kingdom of Didd, where Dr. Seuss's Bartholomew Cubbins lived. I studied the pictures of Bartholomew's little house and the spired houses of the wealthy, the cobblestone streets, and the stone walls with as much intensity as I gave to pictures of the real queen.

Our pretend country had a walled capital city, and the peasants lived in thatch-roofed cottages. I drew countless pictures of them, each with a red geranium in the window. Geraniums were easy to draw. I wasn't a venturesome artist, but I could make geraniums. A cluster of red dots easily suggested a flower. I liked their bright color in the otherwise yellow-brown house. In spite of my interest in peasant houses, I reigned as the queen of Gugog, living in a palace with purple velvet curtains at the windows.

When I played by myself, I was a princess, sometimes dressed in an elaborate ball gown and other times in high-heeled shoes and fancy hats. I always wore gloves. I would wave regally from the balcony over the back porch or receive guests in Grandma's living room, where the furniture became gilded and richly upholstered. Perhaps one of the reasons I thought Grandpa's house was so wonderful was that it always carried a bit of its imagined aura in my mind and was never only another fairly plain faculty home on College Avenue.

Sometimes I, the princess, stood in the front yard to have my picture taken, the stucco house behind me a grand palace. What the neighbors would have seen were bare feet, pigtails, and a cotton dress, but, in my imagination, I wore a billowing white gown with layers of tulle ruffles, lined with snaps. On them I could snap plastic flowers of my choice, purple violets or red roses. One day the dress would be rose festooned and on another day violet. My long, braided hair became short, wavy, and perfectly coiffed. And there were earrings, my pick of roses or violets, to match my dress, or exquisite diamonds, dangling glamorously against my bare neck and shoulders. I must have looked strange as I snapped invisible flowers on rows of thin air and talked to myself, but if someone walked by, I paused in my play until they had passed.

For me, play moved seamlessly between reality and pretending. One moment I inhabited my real world and the next I was some imagined person in an imaginary place. I might be eating off of fine china while my family sat around me using our everyday plates, or I might be in the car riding to town or church, mentally waving to the crowds while I took part in the normal conversation going on around me. Pretending provided a way to explore life outside my own. I could dress in ways not approved in my community, and I could create beautiful surroundings beyond our financial means. And pretend worlds were mine. I could control them and be a star, something I couldn't achieve living on College Avenue in Park View, just a block away from the School.

1 2

Church

WHEN I CAME DOWN the attic steps, Mother was already in the kitchen getting out corn flakes and shredded wheat for breakfast. It was Sunday morning, and we didn't have time for eggs or the fresh squeezed orange juice she sometimes made. We needed to be dressed and ready when Grandpa said it was time to leave. I went down to get my hair combed and found Grandma adding frozen corn to the soup she was making for our midday meal. She put the soup kettle in the fridge and wiped her hands on her apron. She would finish the soup when we got home.

Hair combing on Sunday didn't usually have stories with it because we were all focused on being ready for church. As soon as my hair was braided, I went back upstairs to put on my Sunday dress. I liked its puffy sleeves and belt tied in the back. Mother worked to make the bow even and straight, and then she tied wide satin ribbons on each of my braids, covering the rubber bands that held the braiding in place. Today she chose blue. The blue made my eyes even bluer, she told me with a smile.

Meanwhile Grandpa had pulled his Pontiac out of the garage (which he pronounced to rhyme with *marriage*) and came back inside to call us. He stood at the bottom of the stairs, pulled out his pocket watch like a train conductor, and called up to us, "All aboard! This train leaving in five minutes for Mount Clinton and points west." We came clattering down the stairs in our shiny black patent leather shoes. Mother followed more sedately. Out in the car Jeanie sat on Mother's lap in the front seat with Grandma and Grandpa, while Carol and I sat in the back. We drove around the corner to pick up Mrs. Harper, an elderly woman who rode with us to church. Grandpa tooted his horn and she slowly came down the stairs, supported by her cane. The best part of having her along was that if she thought Grandpa was driving too fast, she poked him with it. This was a joke between them. Grandpa seemed to have an ongoing joke with each person he knew. We were always disappointed if Grandpa didn't get at least one poke on the way to church.

The ride out through the country carried with it the threat of being carsick. My stomach began to feel vaguely detached, as if it were floating around, as we swooped up and down the numerous small hills between home and church, but the ride was too short to make me really sick. By the time we came down the hill into the small town of Mt. Clinton, we were nearly there.

The old brick church sat on a slight hill, surrounded by corn and wheat fields. Inside, it had an acrid smell of old wood and ancient varnish. Like all churches I knew, it was as plain as the old people who attended. There were no pictures, no stained glass windows, no carpet, no candles—just plain wooden benches, frosted glass windows, rubber runners on the aisles, white walls above tongue and groove wainscoting beaded with old amber varnish, and a wooden pulpit on a raised platform at the front of the room. Behind the pulpit was a bench for the pastor. There were two "amen corners": three benches in each of the two front corners, perpendicular to the other benches and facing in toward the pulpit. I often sat there with Grandma on the middle bench of the women's side. One or two old women kept cushions at their favorite spots, but most of us sat on the hard wood. Glass-fronted bookcases stood on either side of the platform, and above the bookcase on the left hung a set of maps of the Holy Land. Grandpa referred to them from time to time in his sermons.

If I sat with Grandma in the amen corner, I couldn't see the maps, but when I sat with Mother on one of the regular benches, I studied the little needle's eye Sea of Galilee connected to the skinny Dead Sea by a line representing the Jordan River—two small blue bodies of water surrounded by tan land. As far as I was concerned, the Holy Land was just that—a tan and barren place, tan like the sand, tan like the ancient buildings and wall around Jerusalem in the pictures Grandpa and Grandma took on their trip.

Church didn't feel quite that barren, but almost. Grandpa's sermon was always based on a Bible text, which he read and then talked about. Much in the sermon passed over my head, but what I did hear was Grandpa's love for God and his vast admiration for the Apostle Paul. This morning he talked about all the things that cannot separate us from God's love. His voice broke and I could see tears in his eyes. At this moment he had my full attention. I didn't understand everything he was talking about; yet I felt myself in the presence of something too important to put into words. If it made Grandpa cry, it was important. Maybe when I grew up, I would feel the way he did. Maybe I would cry too at the thought of God's love, but at this point I was more interested in church being over. Grandpa paused to steady his voice and then proceeded. My mind drifted off again to observing the people around me.

Aunt Elizabeth Grove, an aunt of my father's, kept a cushion on the front bench where she sat. No one else ever took her spot. She was a slight woman whose brown eyes sparkled with quiet passion. One Sunday she spoke up during church, taking issue with a line in a hymn: "Where is the blessedness I knew when first I saw the Lord?" She spoke without invitation and said she couldn't honestly sing those words because she felt closer to God now than when she was first a Christian. Why would the songwriter assume it should be otherwise? I couldn't imagine having the nerve to speak out that way in church or to question the words of a hymn, but since she had done so, I observed her with more interest, always wondering if she would say something like that again.

Mrs. Hartman was even smaller than Aunt Elizabeth but equally spritely and alive. She wouldn't speak up in church, but she wasn't shy. She also sat near the front in order to see. If I told her something she would say, "Wellllll," with the special inflection Virginia people had, expressing interest or sympathy. We were Pennsylvania people and never said *well* like that.

The little "Shantzy babe," as Uncle Bob called the Shantz baby, started to cry. Her mother got up to take her out, but there was no good place to go. We had no nursery. The room behind the sanctuary didn't have solid walls, so the cries were only a little less loud. Mrs. Shantz went outside, but even there the baby's cries came in through the open windows.

Church finally ended. The song leader came to the front and announced the closing hymn. He struck his tuning fork on the lectern and hummed the pitch in his nasal voice. At home we loved to imitate him, but I didn't dare do so at church. Neither did I try to imitate Mrs. Seitz, although I listened for her to slur from one note to another in her alto line. We liked to imitate her too.

I noticed the women more than the men because I had a good view of them from the amen corner. It was harder to watch the men, who all sat on the other side of the sanctuary from the women. I loved to watch people. I knew Grandma watched people too because she sometimes made comments about what she observed, but during church she mostly took notes on Grandpa's sermons. When she wasn't taking notes in her little notebook, her pen added little doodles to the margins of the page.

As usual, Grandpa's car was the last one to pull away from church. He made it a point to talk to everyone. This Sunday he and Dick Good had talked for a long time about plans for summer Bible school. I was hungry and wanted to get home for our midday dinner. It was the best meal of the week, a reward for having sat through church. The rest of the day would be free and relaxed. All the grownups would be around, which meant the possibility of someone reading us stories or pushing us on the swing. I was too old for a nap, but Jeanie still took one, and sometimes Mother did too.

After supper I would have liked to stay in the backyard to play until dark. Instead, we had to go to church again, driving into the sun as it moved toward the western mountains. As I had in the morning, I sat on the hard, wooden bench swinging my legs because they didn't reach the floor. Above me flies made soft static-like sounds as they hit the ceiling tiles and frosted light globes. A regulator clock hanging in the back of the sanctuary ticked loudly as its pendulum swung back and forth.

Since we had no midweek prayer meeting as many churches did, the first part of the evening service was a prayer time, which Grandpa called "a season of prayer." Prayers went on interminably as the congregation kneeled facing backward, toward their benches. I grew tired of the volunteer prayers I couldn't really understand and the long pauses that fell between, while another person gathered up the courage to formulate an acceptable petition to God. Sometimes I quietly drew pictures while kneeling. When Carol and I were younger, we had turned to more mercenary pursuits—playing store. One of us had been the clerk and the other the customer, using Mother's back as a counter. Mother hadn't seemed to mind our buying and selling in "the Lord's House," but when our exchanges became noisy, she stopped us. Being too big to play now, I needed to endure until the end of the prayers. When church was finally over, the twilight was fading into night.

One glorious summer the Brunk tent revivals came to town. For us in quiet Park View it was the equivalent of a circus. The Brunks themselves were not strangers because they lived next door, but revival meetings were a different matter.

When the large tent was erected in an open field on the road to Harrisonburg, we were all excited. It was the summer of 1952 and I was nearly six years old. Going to the revival meetings became a regular part of our lives—we attended almost nightly for several weeks. We had to park in a grassy field and walk quite a distance to the tent where people were gathering. The ground under the hard, metal chairs was covered with wood shavings. Bright lights, loud singing, and forceful preaching created an invigorating theatrical mood that we thrived on, but we took in some of the serious content as well. In her weekly letter to the Lehman family, Grandma wrote, "Each evening when George [Brunk II] calls for those to raise their hands who know they are saved, Kathie's little hand goes up so freely." I watched people go forward during the invitation, knowing I didn't need to. I was confident that all was right between me and God. Grandma noted that one night as we were going to bed, Carol said to me, "Kathie, aren't we glad we're saved?"

She also wrote about the last evening of the meetings when George's brother Lawrence, who led singing, invited young people up to the stage to sing. I doubt that he had in mind children as young as us, but that night Carol and I, along with George's daughter Barbara, who was sitting with us, all went up and stood right under the mic and sang our hearts out. "It must have been a thrill that comes once in a lifetime," Grandma observed.

We played tent meetings at home with Carol being both preacher and song leader and Jeanie and I being the audience. One day, Grandma wrote to the family, "Kathie and Carol had a loud altercation because Kathie said that George says, 'Now we'll have the "invitation"' and Carol said that he says we'll have the 'invocation.'" I threatened not to play if Carol said the wrong word, so Carol bit me on the shoulder. Grandma continued: "That night, [when] George said, 'We'll cast the Gospel net as fishers of men and give the invitation,' Kathie who was standing beside me suddenly turned and with dark blazing eyes said, 'Now I know he says *invitation.*'"

My "being saved" hadn't altered my desire to be right.

13

Starting School

I CLUNG TO MOTHER's hand as we walked up the sidewalk to the front doors of the one-story building that loomed in front of me. I had never been here before, and tomorrow I would be coming alone. Tomorrow I would start first grade.

Today Mother was with me, and we walked up the cement steps together. She pulled open the heavy door. Even without trees for shade, the building was cool inside. It took my eyes a moment to adjust to the dim, windowless hallway. Our footsteps echoed to the end of the hallway and bounced back to meet us. Otherwise, the silence felt immense. I breathed in the smells of sweeping compound, floor wax, and old wood and tightened my grip on Mother's hand. She didn't hesitate. She knew exactly where the first-grade room was because she had gone to this school too.

Park School had been started for the children of the earliest faculty members of Eastern Mennonite School but had then been turned over to the county not many years afterward. It may as well have been a church school, given its lack of diversity. Most students were Mennonite; many of them children of faculty members or administrative staff. The principal was a family friend.

Mother introduced me to Miss Cline, the first and second grade teacher, who stood in the doorway to greet us. I could tell that she was not a Mennonite by the short, curly hair that circled her head like a halo and the pearl earrings and string of pearls she wore. Behind her I could see stacks of new books on the nearest student table. Windows stretched the length of the outside wall, reaching to the ceiling. Below them stood low shelves filled with books.

Mother took this picture on my first day of school.

Miss Cline gave us information about various things, and then came the fun part: walking along the table of books and taking one from each stack. There were a lot of books, and they were all new. I liked their inky smell. I couldn't quite imagine being able to read them, but receiving them was exciting. Already I knew that books were the key to almost everything—and that the first thing to do with a new book was to open it and bury my nose in it for its new-book smell. When we had collected all my books, Mother pulled out her slim purse and carefully counted out the money. I could tell by the look on her face that it was too much— eleven dollars and fifty-eight cents.

I was glad to go back home to the comfort and familiarity of our upstairs living room, where Carol and I sat on the floor to examine my new treasures. I had never had so many new books at once. After Carol and I looked at them, I put the ones I needed for the next day in my red leather satchel along with my prized new pencil case from Uncle Bob. The satchel had been a gift from Grandpa, which I found standing on our kitchen table one afternoon. Never before had I owned anything so red or important-looking. I liked its leathery smell and its two shiny buckles. I had watched Grandpa buckle his satchel many times, and now I had one of my own. A new blue-and gray-lunch box completed my acquisitions. Carol observed everything with awe, maybe even jealousy.

That night I had a bath, and the next morning Grandma braided my hair with extra care. My dress wasn't new, but it had been my summer Sunday dress, so I felt dressed up wearing it on an ordinary day of the week. Mother took a picture of me before I left. Since Carol didn't like to have her picture taken, she didn't mind allowing me the limelight for the moment, but she hovered at the edge, wishing she could be a part of this new adventure.

Phyllis and I set out on our four-block walk to school. We knew the way well: up the street to Mt. Clinton Pike, then past the chapel and along the edge of the campus. Since we were old enough to go to school, we were old enough to walk there alone. Almost everyone did. It would have been unthinkable for any of our parents to accompany us.

Grandma documented my first days at school in her weekly family letter. "Kathie seems very delighted with going to school. Each evening she comes home and says how much she enjoyed it . . . She thinks Miss Cline is the dearest teacher in the whole wide world." But as excited as I was, school felt new and sometimes uncomfortable. I feared making a mistake and being laughed at or scolded. Part of me was on constant guard, but I kept those feelings well-hidden, even from myself.

I liked the routines of school. We stowed our wraps and lunch boxes in closets along the left side of the room and then went to our assigned seats at the tables. Under each place was a cubby hole where we kept our books, pencils, and crayons. We alternated having classes with the second grade. When Miss Cline was with them, we could color, look at books, or do worksheets. Both morning and afternoon, we had recess, when we played on the swings, merry-go-round, and sliding board (slide). Sometimes we played group games.

At noon we went, table by table, to the closets for our lunch boxes and took them back to our seats to eat. When I opened mine, I smelled peanut butter, apple, wax paper, and hints of old milk that never left my thermos. I always had milk to drink with my half sandwich of peanut butter and raisins. I also had celery or carrots, an apple, and perhaps a Fig Newton or Oreo. What was most vivid about lunch was Lois's hard-boiled egg. She may not have had one every day, but when she did, she cracked the shell by hitting it against her forehead, making some joke about her hard head. I imagined it would hurt, so I never tried it myself.

As we finished eating, Miss Cline went to her closet where she carefully freshened her lipstick. We girls watched closely because none of our mothers did that. The nearest any of us came to lipstick were the rare occasions when we had red M&M candies—which we licked and then rubbed on our lips. That red never lasted long because it was too tempting to lick off the sweetness.

After lunch we had rest time, rolling out rugs from home and resting while Miss Cline played music on a little record player. One day she played "Humoresque" by Antonin Dvorak, music I recognized from Grandpa's records. I was amazed at this link between home and the bigger world of school and felt proud, telling Miss Cline that Grandpa had that record too. I could hardly wait to go home to tell Grandpa.

Miss Cline read to us every afternoon, and this was my favorite part of the day. I listened to the story but I also watched her as she read. Everything about her was perfect—her hair, her earrings, her dress, the way she held the book, the way she turned pages, her voice. When I played school at home, I tried to imitate her.

For reading, we took our chairs and made a semicircle facing the blackboard. We started out with letters and sounds and then words. Finally, we were ready for our pre-primer which began, "Look, look, oh look. See Sally, funny, funny Sally." That day I went home, eager to read to Mother. "See, see, oh see. Look at Sally . . ." I read. When Mother pointed out my mistake, I felt deflated. Reading was not going to be as easy as I had hoped.

I was in the lowest reading group, and even there I struggled. Every day I took my reading book home and practiced with Grandma listening, but my reading was halting, bumpy, and uncertain. I wanted to read like Diana, who was different from me. She stood holding her book open, her short hair fashionably waved, and her plaid skirt held out by a crinoline. She read smoothly and at a fast pace. I wished I could be like her. Getting glasses in February made a difference with reading, and I moved to a higher group, but my ugly long stockings and my barely submerged anxiety lingered.

Being shy and awkward made me easy bait for the class prima donna. She reigned supreme in the class, announcing each day whom she liked and didn't like. Some girls rose or fell by her pleasure, but not me. I never rose high enough to fall. A lot of her taunting took place on the playground when the teacher wasn't around and in underground whispers as we ate lunch. Few people escaped her scorn. While that didn't spoil school for me, I still preferred being at home where I could play with my sisters, talk with the grown-ups, or look at books on my own.

I was glad when summer vacation came. It began with Mother graduating from Eastern Mennonite College. She could now look for a teaching job.

14

Iowa

I COULD FEEL THE rumble before I heard it. Then came the light shining on the tracks. Then the whoosh of air as the hurried train pulled into the station. Real trains held little resemblance to the colorful ones in my picture books. Real ones were huge, dirty, noisy monsters. They rushed into the station with a speed and force that I feared would suck me in. I clapped my hands over my ears when the whistle blew and again as the brakes squealed their reluctance to stop. I stared at the dangerous wheels on the metal rails, trying not to think about falling under their sharp edges. The train seemed impatient. It sporadically hissed and quivered as if it could hardly bear to stand still. I watched the conductors in their navy uniforms with shiny buttons and flat-topped hats as they jumped down to the station platform and positioned step boxes for people to disembark. When passengers came down the steps, the conductors offered women a hand or took a suitcase. Men usually got off without any help. All this bustling activity suggested excitement of distant places and different worlds.

Usually when I came to the train station in Staunton, it was to see Grandpa off to one of his many committee meetings or conferences, but this time was different. He had brought us—Mother, Carol, Jeanie, and me—to board the train. He would be the one left standing and waving to us as the train pulled out of the station. Sometimes we drove the long way to Iowa to visit Papa's parents, but this summer we were going by train.

Grandpa, who was an old hand at train travel, joked with the conductor as he helped us find a set of upholstered seats facing each other. He effortlessly stowed Mother's dark blue suitcase onto the rack above our heads before kissing us goodbye. As the train began to move slowly out of the station, we watched through the window, waving to Grandpa as long as we could see him.

Once the train was going full speed and we could see only fields and trees, Carol and I explored. We found the water fountain at the end of the car. It had a holder filled with little cone-shaped paper cups that had a picture of "Chessie, the railroad kitten" printed on the side of each. The bathroom was tiny and its miniature washbowl made us want to wash our hands. Grown-up people sat reading or talking or smoking. I couldn't understand how they could be so calm and disinterested in the midst of such excitement.

We walked up and down the train aisle, getting more drinks than we needed, going to the toilet, coming back to our seats for a bit, and then wandering again. At some point, Mother gave me tracts to hand out. Tracts were small single or double-fold printed leaflets meant to present the gospel in a way that would lead people to become Christians, with titles about sin and salvation and the danger of going to hell. She told me to go to each seat and ask the person whether they wanted something to read. I tried to push aside my shyness and proceed. Some people said no. Others took the tract I offered, with the slightly condescending smile adults reserve for children. It made me squirm. This was something I was supposed to want to do. I believed that it was a good thing because Mother told me to do it, but who was I to interrupt these strangers' lives?

Finally it was dark. We ate our sandwiches, and Mother read us a story before we tried to settle for the night. Carol and I arranged ourselves on one seat and slept in spite of the jostling of the train. Mother had to sit, holding Jeanie's head on her lap. She probably slept less well.

We woke with the sun, all of us except Jeanie. I felt a little groggy, not quite awake, as I looked out the window at a new landscape: flat fields stretching to the horizon, scattered farm houses and barns, no reassuring mountains in sight. If I lived in one of those farmhouses would I be getting up? What would my mother be fixing for breakfast? I imagined eggs and bacon and toast—a good farm breakfast.

Mother looked tired as she sat, still holding Jeanie's head. She didn't want to wake Jeanie, but a woman sitting nearby offered to keep an eye on her so the three of us could go to the dining car. We headed toward our breakfast, steadying ourselves by holding onto seats as we walked. Between cars, I could look down and see slivers of the rails through the connectors and feel the air blowing in the open top half of the doors on either side. The wheels on the tracks made so much noise I couldn't hear my own voice. For those few moments, the train felt as wild and scary as it had when I stood beside it on the platform. Then we would step into the relative quiet of the next car.

I followed Mother into the dining car and surveyed the long lines of little square tables on either side of the aisle. Each was covered by a crisp, white tablecloth and set with silver and large white starched napkins. A waiter led us to a table and handed Mother a menu printed on thick, rich-looking paper. He was dressed in white, just like the waiter pictured in my train book.

Once he left, Mother began perusing the choices. Her eyes went down the list, then up to the top and down again. She sighed and her lips pinched together. She frowned and sighed again. "Everything is so expensive," she said softly. I felt her worry churn in my stomach. What would we do, I wondered? Mother was alone. Grandpa wasn't here to help, nor was Aunt Esther or Uncle Bob. Mother was in an awkward place, and I couldn't come to her rescue.

The waiter came back to take our order. Mother ordered oatmeal for herself and a pot of hot chocolate for Carol and me. The waiter didn't understand. He wanted to bring us each a pot because each held an individual serving. We were small, she explained—we could share one pot. Even to me the order sounded skimpy. I felt apologetic for her.

My confusion and embarrassment dissipated when the waiter returned with our little silver one-cup pot of hot chocolate. I had never seen such a cute pot. Mother carefully poured equal amounts into our thick white cups. The hot chocolate tasted nothing like the milk lightly tinted with cocoa we had at home. This was dark, sweet, and creamy. I drank slowly savoring every swallow, down to the bitter dregs at the bottom.

Soon we returned to the still sleeping Jeanie. I watched as we rode through wide open country. Nothing was quite as exciting as it had been the evening before, so I was glad when we began seeing more houses and then larger buildings and the train began to slow down. We were in Iowa City. As I had anticipated, Grandpa and Grandma Weaver stood on the platform, watching for us—a different Grandpa, a different station. Grandpa Weaver wore his plain suit, and Grandma had on a fine-printed summer dress, the strings of her covering moving gently in the breeze. The conductor helped me down the big steps and I ran into their arms. I was too big to be picked up, but they picked up Carol and Jeanie in turn. We made our way to their black car, all of us walking now and the adults carrying suitcases. Grandpa pulled out of the station onto unfamiliar city streets, but before long we were in the country with fields much like those I had been seeing from the train. Our road turned from blacktop to gravel, and a plume of dust rose behind us. The land flowed in gentle waves, with no mountains to rim the horizon. Finally, I saw the green gables of the familiar white house, shaded by a big tree. The barn and sheds stood beyond it. We were there. Soon uncles and aunts, along with their families, would arrive, and there would be cousins to play with.

In front of Grandpa and Grandma Weaver's house in Iowa, summer 1952. *Left to right:* Grandpa holding Carol, me, Grandma holding Jeanie, Mother. The swing we loved to play on is in the background.

I woke to the sound of the pump squeaking as Grandma pumped fresh drinking water. The pump stood just outside the back door, below our bedroom, and sounds carried clearly through the early morning air. There were voices downstairs—Grandma's soft voice, Grandpa's tenor voice that always sounded to me like it needed a bit of oiling, the aunts' voices strong and lively, the clanking of milk buckets, the clattering of pans and dishes. I lay in bed for a moment feeling the joy of a new day, letting excitement and expectation fill my chest until I could lie there no longer but had to jump out of bed. I shed my light cotton nightgown and slipped into my day clothes, leaving sisters and assorted girl cousins who were still sleeping. I ran down the stairs as quickly as I could so as to minimize the contact of my bare feet on the sharp ridges in the rubber runners. When I burst into the kitchen, an array of smells met me— freshly baked bread, linoleum, gas from the stove, a whiff of stale cistern water, and the permeating smell of milk from the porch sink, where the milk bucket had been washed out and left to dry.

Grandma and the aunts were hurrying to finish up frying eggs and bacon. Along with these came fried potatoes, applesauce, and cookies as well as the bread that accompanied every meal. My sisters and cousins soon appeared, and we all sat down at the kitchen table, with children on a bench on the back side where, from the open window behind us, the new day tickled the backs of our necks. I waited impatiently through a too-long prayer, peeping at the plate of bread and the platter of eggs and bacon. My mouth watered, but I tried not to start giggling or to nudge a cousin. When Grandpa finally finished, the food was passed around. The salty fried potatoes and sweet applesauce seemed strange to me because at home the only things that accompanied eggs were toast and orange juice. We ate large slices of Grandma's soft white bread, spread with real butter, not our usual margarine, and jewel-toned jelly from fruit grown on the farm. Nearly all of the food on the table came from the garden or orchard or barnyard.

Beyond the bountiful breakfast lay the promise of an open day. We played in the front yard under the shade of the big tree, moving Grandma's wooden lawn ornaments—a hen and chicks—all over the yard. We competed, two at a time, sitting on the front porch swing to see who could swing high enough to touch their bare toes to the tongue and groove ceiling. We played circus, gathering the indulgent adults to watch. For a float, we used the old baby buggy frame whose buggy had been replaced by a wooden platform. On washdays Grandma used it to transport her baskets full of wet wash to the clothesline. For us, it became the carriage for our fat man, one of the smaller cousins with a pillow stuffed in his shirt. Kris, the cousin closest my age, helped me push the carriage-float, and the others marched behind, some playing shrill toy flutes from Aunt Virginia's school and others playing mercifully silent pretend instruments.

We spent hours draped over the living room sofa and chairs, listening to Aunt Virginia's records brought home from her classroom for the summer: Burl Ives singing "Shoo Fly" and "I Know an Old Lady (Who

Swallowed a Fly)." We listened to Rogers and Hammerstein's *Cinderella* so often we almost memorized it.

Sometimes I wandered off on my own to explore the musty wash house that smelled of Grandma's homemade soap. I looked at all the odds and ends stored on shelves and in the corners, and I climbed the rickety stairs to the upper room, sure that if I looked long enough, I would discover some treasure.

The Quonset hut in the orchard was filled with the sweet smell of fermenting fruit even though it was empty in early summer. By contrast, Grandpa's workshop smelled oily and was filled with tools, pieces of rope and chain, old tin cans of nails, screws and bolts, oil cans, and who knows what else. Although I didn't understand what he was doing, I stood and watched him work. I always tried to be on hand when he filled the tractor or car with gas because I liked watching the amber gas in the glass bubble on the pump that stood next to the shed.

Most of us cousins made a point of using the outhouse behind the wash house not because there was no other toilet, but because it was a novelty to us. Unlike most outhouses, it smelled of sun-warmed wood, and the seat inside felt smooth from much scrubbing. Sometimes bees buzzing on the hollyhocks outside added a measure of daring to the process. I liked to stand outside the door when no one was around. I would close my eyes, listen to the sound of the breeze and the bees, and feel the warm sun. If I stood there long enough, maybe I could absorb all of summer inside myself and burst with the succulence of it all.

Grandma's large vegetable garden prospered between the house and barn, easily visible from the side dining room window. Behind it a row of grapevines held clusters of not-yet-ripe grapes. In front of the garden, next to the road, Grandma grew a row of gladiolas. Some mornings before it got too hot, she would pick a bunch of them, and I'd watch her quietly place the stems of pink and purple and yellow flowers in a tall glass vase.

I paid little attention to the garden, which was planted between the gladiolas and grapes. I enjoyed the peas, beans, potatoes, and fresh tomatoes that grew there, but it held no special allure. We had a garden at home. I paid even less attention to the animals because I rarely ventured as far as the barn and what lay beyond it. There was at least one cow, giving the milk that arrived each morning on the back porch, and there were chickens, pigs, and sheep.

Grandma's words were few, and when she spoke her voice was soft and a little fuzzy, like my well-worn flannel nightgown. Her laugh was warm and quiet, her smile always a little mysterious, as if she had a private secret she was enjoying. Her laugh was warm though, warmer than the sunny summer afternoon. It brightened the entire room. To me she was beautiful. She stood with dignity, as erect and stately as old Queen Mary in the pictures I pored over in my Queen Elizabeth book. The difference was that Grandma was approachable. Her everyday cotton dress was soft—no silks to wrinkle, no furs to muss, and no hard, sharp jewelry to avoid leaning against. Her smile reflected a quiet, internal peace, not a polite turning up of the lips. I have no specific memory of her talking to me, but I remember clearly moments of quiet when I was the sole recipient of her smile.

One warm, sleepy afternoon, I wandered into the quiet living room. A circle of artificial ivy lay on a doily-covered stand. Always on the lookout for dress-up opportunities, I picked it up and placed the ivy on my head, imagining it to be a hat. Just then, Grandma, with her after-lunch toothpick in place, walked into the room. I was mortified to have been caught acting out my imagination. I feared that she would think I was being silly. Telling her what I was imagining would only make matters worse, because she surely didn't approve of "worldly" things such as hats. But Grandma just smiled at me in the indulgent, loving way grandmothers smile at granddaughters. I guiltily snatched the ivy off my head and returned it to its accustomed place. Neither of us said a word. Grandma left the room, probably still smiling to herself. I, on the other hand, felt chagrinned and told no one. Even so, I didn't doubt her love.

I was sad two weeks later when we departed for home. The cousins had all left by then, and I knew I wouldn't see them for another year or maybe two. Our weeks in Iowa seemed a world apart from Park View, where my ordinary life was lived. We would receive the Weaver family circle letter every so often, which might include pictures, and maybe someone would visit, but that didn't happen often. Our lives would once again center around the School.

15

Augusta County

SOMETHING HAD AWAKENED ME, but I was only vaguely aware of the boom outside. The pounding rain drummed on the tin roof above me, enticing me back toward sleep. "Kathie, Kathie!" Mother's voice was urgent but muffled. Where was she calling from? Not her bedroom next door. Not from the kitchen. I turned over, nested in my upper bunk this Saturday morning, only half awake and still lulled by the rain.

It was September of 1955 and I would soon turn nine. We had just moved to Augusta County, Virginia, almost an hour's drive from Park View, so that Mother could teach in a small church-run school. I was beginning third grade and Carol second. Jeanie would be watched during the day by Mrs. Hackman, the mother of one of the other two teachers who lived next door. She did their housekeeping and, during the week, cooked the evening meal for all of us.

Our house was one of two thin-walled army surplus prefab houses with no space to spare. It had been set up at the edge of the campus just weeks before. Ours consisted of a modest kitchen-living-dining room, a walk-in pantry where a bold wood mouse would later take up residence, a tiny shower room, and two small bedrooms. An oil-burning furnace stood next to the kitchen counter, with an oil tank positioned just behind the house.

"*Kathie!*" Mother's voice finally broke through my fog. "*Kathie, come right away!*" She was *outside*, I realized, *in the rain*. I climbed down my ladder and went to the window where I could see the oil tank lying on its side and Mother standing there, holding her hand over the place where the oil cap should have been. I opened the window a crack. "Bring me the

cork from the big thermos," she called. "*Hurry!*" I went, still in my pajamas, and searched on the pantry shelves until I found the cork. I pulled
on my boots and ran out into the pouring rain. Our house stood in a sea
of mud that made squishy sounds with each step. The ground around it
had been freshly graded after the house was erected. Mother stood in the
downpour, her clothes soggy. She took the cork and jammed it into the
opening, but the pressure was so great that she had to keep holding it in
place. "Go over and tell Mrs. Hackman to call Justus Driver and tell him
the oil tank fell and is spilling oil. He needs to come right away. I can't
keep standing here." Justus was our oil man.

By now I was dripping, too, and shivering in the cold rain. I knocked
on Mrs. Hackman's door, and she answered my knock, still in her housecoat. She looked surprised at such a bedraggled early morning visitor. Before she could even ask a question, I gave her Mother's message. "Come
in," she said. I stood dripping on a rug while she made the call. "Justus
is coming," she reported, and I ran back out to tell Mother and then ran
back into our house. I felt sorry for Justus who had to come out on such
a miserable morning but was relieved for Mother. She looked cold and
alone out there in the rain. I wanted her to come in. I wanted someone
to take care of her.

Before long Justus arrived with his helper, and Mother was able to
come back inside. She was as chilled as she was wet, and she shivered a
long time after she changed into dry clothes. It took even longer for her to
get the smell of oil off her hand, although she washed and rewashed her
hand many times that day. The cork was ruined. We would need to buy a
new one for the thermos.

Although we no longer lived in Park View, Mother knew a lot of people
in our new community. Justus was not just the oil man. He was married to one of Mother's childhood friends who had lived across College
Avenue from her. The school where she taught was bounded on two sides
by the vineyard belonging to her first cousin. Most of the people with
whom we went to church were related to us one way or another. We had
frequent supper invitations that year. The tradition of entertaining teachers in the homes of students was deeply ingrained in this community.
Between school-connected invitations and those of relatives, we visited
more homes than we ever had in Park View.

When Mother had been quite small, Grandpa needed to get rid of their piano. In a rush to some idea of simplicity and humility, the Mennonite Church in Virginia passed a ruling that prohibited pastors from having musical instruments in their homes. Mother had spent her childhood longing to take piano lessons. Finally, the prohibition was removed, but by then she was married and no longer at home. The family legend is that the day the prohibition was removed, Grandpa went to town and bought a piano.

Grandpa wanted to make sure the same deprivation did not befall us, so he bought us our first piano, which we moved into our little prefab home. Carol and I started taking lessons right away. From the beginning I found playing the piano difficult. I needed to pause to think which key to hit, and no amount of practice seemed to make that come automatically. When I felt pressured, I froze. The more I tried, the more mistakes I made. This whole process made me angry, and my anger came out in tears. Mother told me I cried too easily and that I needed to work harder. I couldn't seem to help either the crying or the mistakes.

Carol had no such problem. She passed me quickly, playing with great speed the impressive song, "Riding on a Mule." Her rendition sounded more like a racehorse than a mule. It was mine that sounded like a stubborn, halting mule, but hers was admired, while I needed to practice the song another week. From there she sailed on to the next song while, mule-like, I plodded behind, one, then two, then three songs. Then a whole book. She moved ahead. I faltered.

One late October Friday evening Mrs. Hackman came from next door bringing us news. A plane had crashed near Harrisonburg, killing five people, among them both parents of my friend Helen, whose house on College Avenue I had visited many times. Robert and Mabel were Mother's friends. Papa had worked for Robert's father during his college years, and Mother knew both of their families.

Somehow Carol and Jeanie were gotten off to bed, but I sat on our footstool next to Mother who rocked in the rocker and cried. A familiar, numb feeling pervaded my body. I cried too, thinking of Helen, but mostly, I just sat there knowing I couldn't leave Mother alone with her grief. It grew dark. We heard a car come up the driveway, and then there was a knock at the door. I opened the door and there stood Grandpa and Grandma. They knew Mother would want to come home. Without even asking, they had come to get us. I was relieved. Now I didn't need to keep vigil alone with Mother. We hurriedly packed a suitcase, Mother functioning dully and distractedly. Grandpa carried Carol and then Jeanie to the car in their pajamas for the ride back to Park View.

The next day Mother, Grandpa, and Grandma took me along to visit Robert's parents, who lived down the street, only a block from Grandpa's house. Helen was there, a pale and quiet version of her usually bubbly self. I managed to say something to her, but both of us were at a loss for words. At least she knew I cared, I told myself.

After Christmas my sisters and I got the measles. Jeanie got sick first and was left at Grandma's house to be nursed. The next weekend it was Carol who got to stay. The two of them had a fun week together, but when I finally got sick the following week, I was sicker than both of them together. My stay at Grandma's house was much less fun. Before I was fully well, I came down with conjunctivitis, which meant I stayed even longer. The last week, when both my sisters were back with Mother, our larger world was shaken by the news that five missionary men had been killed in Ecuador. We heard about it on the news. We read about it in the newspaper. *Life* magazine had pages of coverage, showing pictures of the worried wives and their children waiting to learn the fate of the men, pictures of where the men's bodies had been found, and even pictures developed from the camera that belonged to one of the victims, showing several of the people the men had gone to visit.

I felt a connection to these families. They were missionaries as we had been, and they had gone to Wheaton College where Aunt Esther had studied. I looked at the pictures. I studied them, and memorized them, and looked at them again. It felt like our story, my story—the grieving widows, the small children without fathers, the young men whose lives had been cut short. It took me weeks to move beyond being sad.

16

A New House

I WOKE TO GREEN leaves rustling outside my window. The cool night air had freshened the room after the evening's heat. It was summer, my favorite season, and I should have been happy, but it took only moments to remember where I was—not at Grandpa's house, but in the boxy white apartment building down the street. A weight settled in my body, making me want to lie in bed and do nothing because nothing awaited me in the long day ahead. I sat up though, reached to touch the ceiling, and then climbed down the ladder of the bunk bed. Carol was below me, Jeanie in her roll-away. Mother had already gotten up.

In the kitchen she was setting out cold cereal and orange juice for our breakfast. She rushed because she needed to get downstairs to work. "Go call the girls," she told me. "We need to eat right away." It wasn't hard to rouse my sisters. They came in their nightgowns. They could get dressed later. We all sat down. Sun shone in the open eastern window and, with the south window open too, the air moved gently through the room. It wasn't a pretty room like Maple Kitchen in Grandpa's upstairs, but the morning sun made it pleasant.

Mother hurriedly braided our hair, one after another, and then was off down the stairs to the office where she worked. I was almost 10 and old enough to be in charge. Instead of feeling the day spread out deliciously ahead of me as it always had in the past, it stretched out hour after hot and barren hour. The apartment felt empty, and I had little to do other than a few chores—making my bed, washing the breakfast dishes, and maybe ironing handkerchiefs or pillow cases. After that, nothing.

"Do you want to play paper dolls?" Carol asked. "OK," I replied without enthusiasm, going to get the box where I kept mine. Jeanie didn't have any, so I needed to help her find something to do. "Why don't you make breakfast for your doll?" I suggested. At least we had the little green cupboard that held our set of play dishes. Jeanie happily set to work and Carol and I took our paper doll families on a drive in the flashy magazine picture cars we had cut out for them. We brought them back home and changed their clothes. Then Carol's family came to visit mine. Carol's mother scolded her children and said they were so bad they needed to go home right away. "I don't want to play anymore," I said—the truth being I couldn't think of what to do next.

I got out the crayons and my coloring book. Jeanie wanted to color too, so I helped her find her book and we colored for a bit in silence, but that didn't last. Somehow coloring didn't seem as much fun as usual. I liked it more when I was listening to my teacher read a story at school or when Mother or Grandma was around. It was a relief to hear Mother coming up the steps for lunch. With her in the kitchen, life seemed temporarily more interesting, but then she was gone again, and the endless afternoon began.

We got out Chinese checkers. Carol and I put our marbles in place. "Let me play too," Jeanie said, so we waited while she chose a color of marbles and put them in another star tip. The game began well enough, but then Carol tried to jump around a corner, and Jeanie left most of her marbles behind as she took a single marble across the board to her new space. It wasn't fun playing with my sisters when Grandma wasn't there to see that everyone followed the rules and made good moves.

I went downstairs to Mother's office to complain. "There's nothing to do upstairs," I whined. "Carol and Jeanie don't play right. When will you come home?"

"You girls need to go outside for a while. You can't stay in all day," she said.

"There's nothing to do outside."

"You need to find something. You need to be outside for at least a half an hour."

"That's too long! There's nothing to do."

"You can find something. Now go!"

I felt like I was being punished, sentenced to time in the yard. I hated the tiny, almost bare space around the apartment building. It held no interesting nooks or crannies, nothing to inspire my imagination. The only sidewalk went from the front stoop to the road, not long enough for skating or bike riding. We didn't play ball and there weren't group games that worked well for three people, especially when the two others were my infuriating little sisters. I sat on the stoop and pouted. Mother was completely unreasonable. She was unfair. If I had known any swear words, I would have used them, but I didn't, so I sat feeling angry. As far as I could tell, this afternoon was endless and empty and I, on principle, could think of absolutely nothing to do. My chest felt hot and stuffy, and I wanted to squirm or scream. My cheeks flamed. I itched all over. Carol was mad too. She thumped around under the lone tree. Jeanie wanted to be pulled in the wagon so I pulled her for a bit, but the ground was bumpy and she soon tired of that. Finally, the front door opened. Mother stood there. Her work day was over and we could come in.

We had returned to Park View at the end of our year in Augusta County and had moved into this apartment. We could no longer live at Grandpa's house because Uncle Bob and his wife Ruby now lived in our old space. I adored Aunt Ruby. She was different from Mother, Aunt Esther, and Aunt Dot, who were more conventional and ordinary. Aunt Ruby brought something fresh and new to our family. When she and Uncle Bob had moved in a year earlier, I had watched with great interest as she unpacked her almost new wedding gifts, things prettier and newer than ours, but what I liked most about Aunt Ruby was the way she dressed. She didn't wear cape dresses but interesting clothes that didn't follow the rules— skirts and blouses and short-sleeved dresses that didn't look plain at all. Her most impressive outfit was a turquoise maternity top that had black buttons with rhinestone centers. These were as close to jewelry as anyone in my family ventured. If I could have, I would have taken some of those buttons to make pretend earrings.

I also loved my little cousin Judy, who was a year old when they moved to Park View. She reminded me of a baby robin when I first saw her: her dark hair was short and close to her head like a wet baby bird. I was too young to babysit her, but I could play with her when we visited.

Our summer apartment had the advantage of being upstairs from Mother's new secretarial job, but compared to Grandpa's house, it seemed impoverished. We didn't have the books and magazines, or the music and outdoor space I had always taken for granted, and since it was temporary, we had not completely unpacked. Everything seemed tentative and unsettled. For the first time in my life, Mother was gone all day, and we three were home alone.

In spite of my foggy boredom, life was not as grim as I made myself believe it was. Five o'clock would come. I'd hear Mother's steps on the stairway and know I could suspend my boredom until the next day. After supper we often drove to the north end of Park View, beyond the college campus, where the paved part of College Avenue turned into a dirt extension. There, next to a scrappy locust tree and a cow pasture, our new house was rising from the limestone-layered hill, the same hill on which the School and Grandpa's house stood. To the east, beyond the cow pasture, stood a faded red barn and white farmhouse. Farms and fields stretched all the way across the valley to Massanutten Mountain.

Our house was a dream come true for Mother. She and Uncle Bob had bought adjacent lots a year earlier, but even before then, she had spent many evenings with a ruler and pencil, drawing house plans and revising them over and over again. I learned by heart the things she valued: a big picture window facing the eastern mountains, oak floors and woodwork, plenty of closets and storage space. She arranged and rearranged rooms and closets and the chimney so that every square inch could be used. Now, when her long days of work were over, she was eager to check the progress of her dream.

At first, we saw only the cement slab—not interesting—but then cinderblocks formed the basement rooms, and before long we could walk on subflooring for the first story. A real house was taking shape before our eyes. My interest increased as the studs went up. The house looked more and more real. I liked walking around in this newly created space, picking up odds and ends—sawed-off pieces of wood, bits of wire, whatever waste was left lying around. I could begin to imagine the rooms and where we would place furniture. I particularly took delight in walking through future walls. It seemed daring, almost magic, to go from one room to another without using doorways.

Once the walls and windows were in place, the time came for the fun decisions, the ones I wanted to be part of. I spent a great deal of time going through the ring of Formica samples for the kitchen counter. I wanted something exciting that looked like kitchens in the women's magazines I perused at our piano teacher's house while Carol and Jeanie had their lessons. Mother listened to my suggestions but then calmly went on to choose what she wanted—a more conservative pattern called "green linen." I thought her choice looked nice, but I was disappointed that our kitchen wouldn't look modern.

The move to our new house happened on a Friday, Columbus Day, in 1956. The house itself was finished but so new that much remained to be done. A wooden sidewalk led across the muddy yard to temporary wooden steps at the front door. We had no shades or curtains at our windows, and no tiles on the bathroom wall. The kitchen cupboards had not been varnished. Our piano would not arrive for several weeks.

Because Mother had to work every day and do housework evenings and weekends, she had little time for finishing up the new-house projects. She felt discouraged by all that still needed to be done. Curtains were a priority, especially for the picture window where the sun poured in each morning. She took the time to choose fabric, and then one day women from church came to make the curtains. I came home from school to find fabric draped everywhere and women laughing and talking as they worked. One portable sewing machine stood on the dining room table and another on a card table in the living room. I watched the women sew lining to the backs and pleating tape along the top of each curtain. They had brought food for supper, so the party atmosphere continued into the evening. The curtains didn't get finished by the time everyone had to leave, so Aunt Ruby finished them up, and then I got to help slip the pleating clips into the slots of tape along the top of each panel. I counted carefully the number of slots between clips to make even spacing between the perfectly formed pleats. When we were finished, I surveyed the neat, even pleats with great satisfaction. They looked perfect, just like magazine pictures.

That fall Aunt Esther lived with us. Grandma and Grandpa were in Philadelphia for Grandpa's sabbatical, and other people rented their house. I felt more secure with Aunt Esther around. She was almost a second mother. In one of her letters to Philadelphia she wrote, "I've been able to stay and see the girls off, kiss them, finish Carol's dishes, assist Kathie with the lunch, comb Kathie, clean the house up etc.—most of which would take me no longer to do all by myself, but I'm trying to help them learn to do their jobs."

In another letter she wrote about one evening after school:

> [Carol] just felt so very bad because she didn't know how to do her [arithmetic] problems. I asked her what kind of problems they were and she showed me 104—62 . . . When I showed her how to do it, she said she must have gotten all of hers wrong . . . I proposed going up to my classroom and getting the 3rd grade book like hers and helping her. [Aunt Esther's curriculum library contained complete sets of text books from various publishers.] So, after supper we had quite an arithmetic session which ended up in her doing them all o.k. Also K. was feeling bad about not knowing her adding and subtracting facts, so I worked with her on some.

I could tell, by her barely submerged smile, that Aunt Esther was enjoying the teaching session. She, like Grandma, was a born teacher.

We used this picture for Christmas cards the first year we were in our new house. I am pouring tea for Carol, Mother, and Jeanie (*left to right*)**. The new curtains I helped to pleat are behind us.**

Our house became the center of family life once we all moved there. Aunt Esther slept upstairs in one bedroom and my sisters and I slept in the other one; Mother was on the first floor. Uncle Bob and Aunt Ruby and their two children lived in the basement apartment. We didn't walk in and out of their apartment the way we did at Grandpa's house, but we went there often. Every morning Judy, who could still barely talk, would come up the stairs after breakfast to ask for the Morgen Zeitung (morning newspaper), which we shared, and we all used Uncle Bob and Aunt Ruby's phone as needed. We frequently ate meals together and celebrated birthdays as a group, either upstairs or down.

Letters hint at how tasks seemed to flow back and forth between families. Mother watched the "least ones" when Aunt Ruby went to see Uncle Bob play basketball. Aunt Esther cleaned our kitchen and dining room floors and waxed them. For my birthday party with school friends, Aunt Ruby drew a donkey and made tails for "pin the tail on the donkey," and she baked a cake for the family dinner we had later that evening. Uncle Bob sat down with Mother to help figure out the complexities of calculating taxes with renters in the house.

Finances were not communal, but those who could helped those in need. When Mother got an unexpectedly high bill—$700 instead of the $200 she anticipated—she wrote to Grandpa in Philadelphia saying "I just don't have it. *What shall I do?*" She had only six dollars left in her checking account after paying regular bills. He must have sent her a check, because in the next letter she thanked him. She already owed money to Uncle Bob, and both she and Uncle Bob borrowed money from Aunt Esther, who extended generous interest-free loans.

After Christmas, Aunt Dot and Uncle Bob Yoder and their three children moved from Indiana into Grandpa's house so Uncle Bob Yoder could go to college. This meant that there was another family with whom to share tasks and events. Mother babysat for Aunt Dot, and Aunt Dot picked us up from school on rainy days. Once the weather turned warm, we had picnics almost every week. We sometimes gathered on the hill behind the School, where we could see mountains to the east and to the west. Other times we went to Park Woods, just beyond Park School. I felt secure in the circle of family members, sitting around our hotdog fire, or in the cluster that stood watching the pink glow of the sunset. I belonged. Unlike our small, fractured household, all of us together were a whole and complete unit, picnicking on the campus of the School, which was our even larger family. I felt fortunate to be a part of all this. There was no other family quite like it in the whole world.

17

Philadelphia

FAIRLY WELL SETTLED IN our new house, we could finally think beyond curtains and seeding the lawn and new shrubbery. All year Grandma had told us about the wonders of Philadelphia. She really wanted us to come for a visit during our Easter break. We were equally eager. I had never been in a large city before, except for my brief trip with Uncle Bob to meet Grandpa and Grandma in New York City after their European trip. That didn't really count, since I had been only five years old. Now I was 10 and ready for a big city adventure.

I carried in my mind the pictures from *Thee Hannah*, which was set in Philadelphia. Of course, the city would look different now than it had one hundred years ago, but Independence Hall was still standing, and the Liberty Bell was there. I wanted to see Betsy Ross's house because I had read the story of her making the first flag, and I also wanted to see the present-day sights. Grandma had given vivid descriptions of the places she went, especially Wanamaker's department store.

Carol and I had read about John Wanamaker in one of the *Childhood of Famous Americans* series, and now we would get to go to the large, fancy store he built. Grandma went there to sightsee as much as to shop, riding the escalators up and down between its many floors and looking at things she could never afford to buy. The store had a large organ on which recitals were given and elaborate Christmas decorations. Now, at Easter, two large paintings hung in the central area: *Christ before Pilate* and *Christ on Calvary* (by Mihály Munkácsy). She wanted to be sure we saw them. Religious displays in public places seemed a marvel to me. Bible stories belonged to my small world, not the world of the fashionably dressed people dashing around in a glittering city department store.

We arrived at Grandpa's apartment on Friday night, just in time for supper. It seemed strange to see them in an unknown place that smelled different from their house in Park View. We ate supper on strange dishes in a room with strange furniture, but Grandma and Grandpa were familiar. I was so excited I could hardly eat. After supper we talked about what we would do the next day. Grandma warned Carol, Jeanie, and me repeatedly that it was important not to talk with strangers or to go off with them. Apparently, the city was filled with not only strangers, but suspect strangers who might turn out to be kidnappers. I planned to be careful.

The next morning after breakfast, we took off with Grandma, leaving Grandpa to his work. Wanamaker's lived up to my expectations—big and overwhelming. The paintings looked dark to me and too high to study in detail. Grandma bought new skirts for Carol and me, which I insisted on carrying in a shopping bag, even though I had to hold it up to keep it from dragging on the floor. That proved tricky when we got to the escalator. As I was trying to manage the new experience of stepping onto moving stairs, holding the rail with one hand and the bag in the other, a strange man dressed in a suit smiled at me and asked if he could hold it for me. I shook my head no, but Grandma said, "Let him help you." I couldn't understand. Here was a strange *man*, offering to take my bag. If I gave it to him, what would stop him from running off with our precious purchases? "Go on," Grandma said, so I handed the bag to him, bracing for him to bolt. Instead, he held it all the way up and then, smiling, handed it back to me. I was equally relieved and confused. Why, after all the warnings, had Grandma thought it OK for me to surrender my bag? I wondered what she saw that let her know he was a safe person. I surely couldn't tell. Maybe the city wasn't as dangerous as she led me to believe.

On Easter morning, Carol and I woke before anyone else. There wasn't a lot to do, so we decided to take a little walk outside. As quietly as we could, we went down the stairs to the first floor, unlocked the door, and walked out onto the street. It was early. No one was out, and cars were few. We walked to the corner, turned, walked the next block, and turned again until we had circled the block. We let ourselves back in and up the stairs to Grandpa's apartment where we were met by three upset adults. Where had we been? Didn't we know that going out alone was dangerous? We were not to do that again! I was thoroughly puzzled. Our walk had seemed perfectly safe to me. We had seen no one. We had carefully walked in a square so as not to get lost. Why was this so awful when it was OK for me to give my shopping bag to a stranger? The rules of city life baffled me. Neither of us felt repentant. Our independent walk had been our own adventure, and the realization that the adults were dismayed only added to our sense of accomplishment. I knew we had been perfectly safe. We had proven them wrong.

Back in Park View, Carol and I proudly wore our new skirts to school. They were cut in a circular pattern so that they hung in ripples, but more wonderful was the nylon netting underskirt that held the fabric in perfect convolutions. I turned up the edge of the skirt to show my friend Pat the netting as we walked to school. Even she didn't have a skirt as fancy as mine. No matter how commonplace life in Park View might seem, there was always Philadelphia glittering in the distance—and my skirt to prove it.

18

When I Grow Up

I STOOD HOLDING MY breakfast dishes, ready to carry them to the sink. Mother, still in her housecoat, ran the brush through Jeanie's straight hair and glanced up at the clock hanging above the refrigerator. I looked too—eight o'clock. Almost time to leave for school.

"It wasn't supposed to be like this. I never wanted to have a job," Mother said. "I just wanted to stay at home and be a housewife." Bitter disappointment seeped in and around her words and filled the air between us. "This isn't what I wanted," she said as she pinched her lips and braided silently.

I didn't move. A familiar weight filled my chest, a tearless grief for which I had no words, a pain that radiated in all directions. Surely there should be some comforting thing to say to her, but I didn't know what it was. I glanced at the clock again and moved toward the sink.

"Can you put milk in the thermoses?" Mother asked, as if her previous statements had not happened. I silently got out the milk bottle and filled our three lunch box thermoses, checked that we had napkins, and snapped each box closed.

By then Mother had put a rubber band on Jeanie's braid and rushed off to dress and comb her own hair. I had my books gathered by the time she reappeared, her usual put-together self. Her dress fit well, her hair was pulled back into a neat bun, and her covering was pinned in place. She carried with her the faint fragrance of Quaintance, the Avon sachet she always dabbed on her wrists. And she had put on her usual pleasant face—the one she wore most of the time, the one her students and colleagues would see, the one Jeanie remembers most clearly. I too covered my feelings with a smile as I waited for Carol and Jeanie to get their lunch boxes. We walked out the door together.

It wasn't just Mother's sense of loss that kept those moments alive in my memory. Somewhere inside a seed had been sown. I didn't say the words to myself, but the message was planted: staying home with children was the ideal. Working elsewhere was secondary, only a backup plan.

19

Music

IN OUR FAMILY MUSIC was next to God—not godliness, but God. And "music" meant classical music, along with hymns. Gospel songs, with their rollicking choruses and questionable theology, were allowed reluctantly, although I secretly enjoyed them. *Jazzy* was a derogatory term, and popular music we considered completely lacking in taste; Elvis Presley with his slicked back hair and sexy moves was downright sinful. The names of movie stars were not familiar to us, but Bach and Schubert and Tchaikovsky were household names, and we knew all about Robert Shaw, Dietrich Fischer-Dieskau, and Arturo Toscanini. As teenagers we were, in fact, more than a little snobbish. When someone mispronounced a musical name or term, it indicated their lack of class.

At Grandpa's house we had heard music every day. When we were small, stacks of thick 78 rpm records dropped one by one to the turntable and played symphonies and concertos, one movement per disk. "Listen to this," Grandpa would say. "This is called the *Surprise* Symphony. Shhhh . . . Hear how soft the music is." His eyes would twinkle. He stood with his finger to his lips and then would laugh when the loud chord came. "Joseph Haydn wrote lots of other symphonies," Grandpa explained, "and lots of pretty music." He played Handel's *Concerti Grossi*, explaining to me that *concerti grossi* was the plural of *concerto grosso*, a random fact I had little use for but felt great satisfaction in knowing. He told me how Handel's *Water Music* had been played for the king of England while he floated down the Thames on a big barge and that the king kept asking for it to be played over and over again. I imagined myself on the barge, dressed royally, listening to the music float out over the water, which rippled darker and darker as evening turned to night.

Occasionally on Sunday afternoons, Grandpa invited students to come to his house for music. They arrived, carrying brown paper bag lunches the dining hall provided for their Sunday evening meal. Twenty or more people might arrive in twos and threes. Grandpa welcomed them at the door with his hearty handshake and ushered them in. I stood in the background watching as the laughing, chattering students filled the sofa and chairs and spilled onto the living room carpet and even sometimes the linoleum of the study. Grandpa stood next to the Victrola, as he always referred to his record player, and introduced the music he was going to play—an oratorio like Haydn's *Creation* or Mendelssohn's *Elijah,* or one of Bach's passions. I had the job of handing out the purple mimeographed sets of words.

While the music was important to him, he was equally interested in the words and wanted everyone to understand how music and words enhanced each other. Many students had come from Mennonite communities where higher education was suspect and the arts viewed as irrelevant, if not a frivolous extravagance. Such ostentation had no place in the simple, separate-from-the-world life we espoused. This meant that classical music, in any context, was a new experience, and Grandpa wanted to ensure that it be a good one.

I listened diligently to what he told the students. Some of his commentary was hard for me to understand, but some I understood. When he introduced Bach's Mass in B Minor, he told us that he had wondered why phrases (of words) were repeated over and over again. "I think that Bach is saying these words are important and he wants us to reflect on them." I would guess now that it had as much to do with the baroque style of music, but that Grandpa saw it primarily as a meditative invitation fits with the spirit of Bach and speaks to Grandpa's own deep spirituality. He talked about the music too, pointing out how Haydn used instrumental lines in *The Creation* to suggest whales and worms.

The listening began. The students sat quietly except for the rustle of turning pages. I would be determined to listen to the entire oratorio, but after a few pieces my interest flagged. It was hard for me to follow the words, especially if the performance was in German or Latin and we were following a translation. I wouldn't have admitted it, but the music bored me a little too—especially those tedious arias that, as Grandpa said, went on and on, repeating the same words over and over again. I would wander out to the kitchen and then back again. I marveled at how the students could sit so quietly and listen. I was relieved when Grandma called me to the kitchen to help set out glasses on a tray for the grape juice and lemonade mixture she made to go with the student lunches.

Finally, the music ended. Grandpa might make a few comments and ask questions to encourage discussion. The students opened their lunch bags, joking about what kind of sandwiches they had and trading food with each other. One of my sisters passed out napkins, Grandma and Aunt Esther served grape lemonade, and I followed with Ritz crackers. I loved this part of the afternoon because I could sit and listen to the students talk. The students seemed grown-up but not as serious as my adults were. We didn't laugh and tease and say funny things nearly as much as they did. The students clearly liked and respected Grandpa and called him Brother Chester. I felt proud that he was my grandpa.

20

Baptism

THERE HAD NEVER BEEN any question in my mind that I would "become a Christian." In fact, I had always thought of myself as a Christian. I wanted to be good and, if intentions counted, I was in a general sense Christian, even though I often fell short.

Becoming a Christian was a rite of passage, though, something that had to happen before one could be baptized and become a member of the church. While it was as natural a part of growing up as getting permanent teeth, I knew I needed to go through the formal process. The only question was when.

Virtually every adult in my life was Christian. I didn't know anyone personally who would have said they weren't. We looked askance at those outsiders whom we considered non-Christian, people like Mr. Hopkins, who was a "drunkard," and people who committed crimes. Others seemed marginal—the relatives who had left the Mennonite Church, those who smoked or drank or wore jewelry. That they still considered themselves Christian puzzled me. Maybe there were tiers in Christianity. If so, we were surely in the top tier.

The summer before third grade, my mother, sisters, and I spent a month in West Virginia, living with the Seitz family, while Mother and five or six others taught summer Bible school at various churches. Bible schools generally lasted two weeks and were held either in the morning or the evening. Some weeks, the teachers went to one church in the morning and another in the evening. They were busy every day, but Carol, Jeanie, and I—along with Eunice Seitz and her younger sister—filled the long summer days with play.

The Seitz family had lived near Mt. Clinton and had gone to church with us for years. Eunice and I had played together and were in the same Sunday school class. Every Sunday morning, when we drove by their white farm house, surrounded by apple orchards, Grandpa would honk his horn, and we would look to see if they were getting into their wood-paneled station wagon.

Now the Seitzes lived in West Virginia and we didn't see them often, so being with them for a whole month was a treat. We and all the teachers ate our meals with them at a long dining table and joined their family routines, which included worship after breakfast. I would have preferred not to be included in that particular ritual, but that was not an option. We sat in a crowded circle in the living room. Someone read from the Bible and made comments. Then we all kneeled at our seats for prayers, which seemed to stretch on forever.

When worship was over, we were finally free. We spent hours on the rocky riverbank behind their house playing clinic, inspired by the next-door medical clinic staffed by Dr. Bucher, whose daughter also played with us. Other times we rowed a small boat on the mill stream in front of their house or sang with the portable organ one of the teachers had brought along. The adults laughed and joked a lot. I wished all of life were this much fun.

Revival meetings were held at one church along with Bible school. One night when the invitation was given, Eunice and I both raised our hands indicating that we wanted to become Christians. The next morning, I woke with sun shining in on the quilt that covered my bed, feeling new and clean. I was now part of the church—part of something much bigger than me. It was as if my life were starting over again in a fresh way.

Because I was only eight, Mother, Grandpa, and Grandma thought it wise to wait several years for baptism. I was disappointed because Eunice was going to be baptized almost right away, but as time went by, I didn't think of it often and then all but forgot about it.

Then, four years later, as my friend Barbara and I rode our bikes in loose circles on the wide street beside the School's chapel, she asked me, "Why don't you get baptized? Pat and I are." Pat was the neighbor with whom I usually walked to school. I felt awkward talking about baptism. As central as church and faith were to my life, speaking personally about such things made me uncomfortable. Adults talked about faith in their grown-up, coded language, but we children didn't.

Despite my unease, I told Mother that I wanted to be baptized. To my irritation, she asked Carol if she also wanted to be baptized, and Carol said yes. This was supposed to be my event, my moment to move ahead on my own without Carol trailing me, but no such luck. Even worse, Mother called Grandpa and Grandma, who came right away to talk with us. This felt really awkward. Choosing to be baptized was one thing; talking about it another. I felt like I was parroting someone else's words. I wanted to squirm or scream or run away. Instead, I repeated to Grandpa and Grandma what I had told Mother.

I didn't look forward to baptism or the foot washing that I would have to take part in when we had communion, but Mother signed us up for membership classes to be held at the home of our bishop. It was his role to conduct instruction classes for the congregations under his care. Dawn, who was also from Mt. Clinton, was part of the class along with people from other churches. We used a small catechism book, learning the answers to a list of questions.

One evening I disagreed with the bishop on one of the answers. He asked me what a person must do to become a Christian, and I replied with one of the many verses we had memorized: "If we confess our sins, he is faithful and just to forgive us our sins, and to cleanse us from all unrighteousness." (I John 1:9 KJV) He replied that this was for people who are already Christians. Confessing Jesus as Lord was the answer he wanted. I saw no reason why my verse couldn't equally apply, but I kept my thoughts to myself. I knew I shouldn't question a church leader. Neither did I bring it up at home because I feared I might be told I was wrong. I liked my own interpretation and didn't want to surrender it to anyone.

Besides taking membership classes, we had another preparation to make: buying coverings. Being baptized meant that we would now wear them every day. At least this part of the process was interesting. Mother took Carol and me to Martin's store to look at coverings arranged in the big drawer next to the handkerchiefs. I was glad we didn't need to wear big, old-lady coverings but could choose from among smaller ones that covered less hair. We avoided the smallest ones, which we viewed with scorn tinged with envy. They were for people who tried to appear as if they wore no covering at all, not serious people like us.

On the baptism Sunday, I bowed my head enough that the water didn't run down my face. The bread-and-grape juice part of communion was fine, but I found the foot washing we practiced as part of communion less comfortable. Our foot washing, done in pairs, was modeled on Jesus' washing his disciples' feet at the last supper. It was a sign of being willing to do a humble service for another. That mostly passed me by because Dawn and I planned to wash each other's feet so we could avoid washing feet with someone we didn't know well or didn't like. While I was sincere in my baptismal vows, I felt no particular joy, no clearer commitment as a result of the service. The mechanics of each part had claimed my attention, and I sighed with relief when it was over.

Now that I was baptized and wore a covering, I could "put up" my hair like high school girls did. Pat still had pigtails sometimes with her covering, but once I began to put up my hair, I didn't want to go back to my little girl style. I wrapped my braids around my head and pinned them in place with hair pins that often irritated my scalp. Some days I feared the braids would slip down. I knew my hair looked messy and it felt uncomfortable. Baptism, rather than being an entry into a new life, seemed an initiation into discomfort and self-consciousness—the fellowship of the awkward and unattractive.

During upper elementary school and high school, I occasionally found myself questioning how it was that I was fortunate enough to have been born into a family and church that held the one true faith (Christianity) and also interpreted the Bible accurately. How could we be so sure we were right? How, of all the people in the whole world, was it that we were the only ones who had the truth, who lived the right way? Why would God give the truth only to a small group of people and seemingly ignore the rest of the world? Even saying that it was our job to spread the gospel made little sense. Why would God parcel out the truth in such a stingy way, knowing many would die not knowing it?

On the other hand, what if another religion was right and we were wrong? Just because we believed the Bible to be true, did that make it so? What if I had been born into a Hindu or Muslim culture? Their beliefs, of which I actually knew very little, made no sense to me, but I wondered if my beliefs—the virgin birth, Jesus' miracles, and his resurrection—might seem equally strange and unbelievable to them.

In spite of those troubling questions, I would settle back into the beliefs with which I was surrounded. No one I knew questioned the truth or normalcy of Christianity or our specific beliefs. I never heard them challenged in a serious way by someone with a different worldview. Yet those niggling thoughts surfaced from time to time. I'd question but then fall back into being thankful that I was born in the right faith and could rest in its comfortable certainty.

21

High School Years

I CROUCHED DOWN ON the bare cement floor, between a cinder block wall and the toilet. I was missing the class going on upstairs. Black waves rolled over my vision. For a second or two, I couldn't see. Then bright bursts, like a flash camera going off, then more black waves. I curled over in agony. If I stood up, I feared I might faint. I'd never fainted before, but this must be how it felt. It was time for the smelling salts delicate women called for in the some of the novels I read.

My menstrual cramps had never been this bad before. Today they came in a constant flood, relentless, never-ending, like my gut was turning inside out. Nothing else really mattered. I just wanted this all-consuming pain to go away. Why did it need to happen in my first week of eighth grade?

I didn't know what to do. I wanted to be at home. I wanted Mother to be there—to stand beside my bed and bring me a hot water bottle, to tuck the covers around me, maybe put on a favorite record. Instead, I was alone in this ugly, windowless room. No one else was in the basement, and no one was likely to come down during class. It worried me that I couldn't make it upstairs to tell the teacher why I had disappeared. I feared I would faint if I tried, and besides, I didn't want anyone to see me. I knew my face was bleached. That always happened when cramps got this bad. If I did make it upstairs, what could I say in front of the boys? And how could I ever make the ten-minute walk home? I'd have to walk, of course. That's how I got to school, but I didn't know if I could manage it now. Mother was teaching. She couldn't leave class to drive me home.

The pain is vivid in my memory, but the happenings around it thin out and disappear. I got home somehow and spent the rest of the day lying in bed, but by then the worst was over. The house was safe and quiet except for the purr of the furnace, and I dozed off into oblivion. I had retreated for the moment from everything new I was facing.

Change terrified me, and any new situation triggered a sense of being alone, as if I were in a wilderness that offered me no resources. Ironically, little was new to me on this familiar campus with teachers I knew and friends I'd had since grade school. However, there was one major difference. Until this point, I had been a visitor on the campus that belonged to the adults in my life—Mother, Aunt Esther, Uncle Bob, and Grandpa— who moved around with confidence. They had offices and mailboxes, colleagues and students. Now I needed to inhabit their world in my own right. I wasn't sure I was up to it. Did I really belong? Could I belong? I needed to begin walking the hall of the Ad Building as a student, not as a barefooted girl coming to get the family mail. I was now expected to sit in chapel like the almost grown-up juniors and seniors, who seemed so casual and happy, laughing and joking with each other. I couldn't fathom being one of them. I didn't know if I'd ever feel easy in this bigger world. My barefooted and pigtailed self, like the phantom limb of an amputee, felt present even in its absence. I simply couldn't translate myself into a high school student. My cramps were the only thing that penetrated the numb fog of that first week of school, the only thing I really felt.

Reading was my passion. I was rarely without a book. If I had free time in school, I read. When I came home after school, I read. I read on the toilet. I tried to squeeze in a few pages of reading at night before I turned out the light. I read almost anything—biography, fiction, historical fiction.

One summer evening in early high school, our friend Kathie came to visit Carol and me. We were just being introduced to classic novels in our English classes and were intoxicated by the new world before us. We carried a stack of books to a table on the small balcony above our side porch. We would discuss those books, we decided. We hoped for an intense, enlightening conversation, but the reality fell far short. We had no idea how to have the kind of discussion we desired. We flipped pages, made prosaic comments about why we liked a given book, took deep breaths of longing, and meandered. When it was no longer light enough to see, we gathered our books and went inside. I felt let down and disappointed. I could taste my longing and the emptiness of our inability to probe the world of literature. It hung enticingly beyond us but out of reach.

It had been an ordinary October Monday, a day of school and homework. As I gathered my books to head upstairs for bed, I was thinking about my upcoming birthday when I would turn fifteen—the age at which Mother said I could start drinking coffee. The ring of the phone broke into my thoughts. I glanced at the clock—10:15. Who could be calling so late? Mother answered in the den, and I paused, curious. Mother wasn't saying anything, so I went toward the door. "Both of them?" I heard Mother ask. She was sitting at her desk, holding the receiver and writing in shorthand on a scrap of paper. She always used shorthand when she had lots to write down. She said something about a funeral. She offered to call Goldie, Papa's sister. Something was wrong, terribly wrong—but what? Finally, Mother hung up and turned to Carol, Jeanie, and me. By then we were all standing in the doorway. "Girls," she said, "that was Uncle Dean in Iowa. He had some sad news. Grandpa and Grandma Weaver were both killed in a car accident today." We stared at Mother. "They were on their way home from [cousin] Twila's wedding in Kansas. That is all Uncle Dean knows right now."

I walked over to stand next to Mother. She had begun shivering as if she had chills. I didn't know what to do or say. How could this be true? We had just been talking about going to Grandma and Grandpa Weaver's for Christmas. I felt like I was acting a part in a well-rehearsed, drama— one we had been through before.

Mother picked up the receiver and dialed Grandpa's number. I heard him answer and without any preface she began, "Papa, Dean Yoder just called to tell us that both Papa and Mama Weaver were killed in a car crash today on their way home from Kansas."

"Oh . . . oh, my . . ." Grandpa responded. "We'll be right over." His strong voice carried loudly enough for me to hear. I was relieved they were coming. Mother continued to shake, even as she ran her slender finger down the list to Aunt Goldie's number.

"Hello?" I heard Aunt Goldie's familiar voice answer. I wished I could protect her from the news a few minutes longer, but Mother didn't pause.

"This is Miriam and I have some sad news . . . Dean called to say that both of the folks were killed in a car accident today on the way home from Kansas." Aunt Goldie gasped. There was silence and then she started to cry. "Is Mel there?" Mother asked. "I can talk to him." This wasn't fair, I thought. Mother had no one else to take over for her, to hold things together so she could fall apart. She had to do it all.

I heard the front door open and the three of us rushed to greet Grandpa and Grandma while Mother finished talking with Uncle Mel. Grandpa's strong arms held me tight. What would I do without him? "My, we didn't expect to hear such sad news tonight," Grandma said as she hugged me, and I let tears come. There was now someone else to take over. Mother joined us and both Grandpa and Grandma hugged her. We huddled together in the middle of the living room feeling the comfort of each other's presence.

Mother told Grandpa and Grandma the little she knew, and then Grandpa went to the den to call a brother of Grandma Weaver and a sister of Grandpa Weaver, both of whom lived nearby. The rest of us sat in the living room trying to take in the enormity of the news. We talked about the funeral and who might be able to go. It cost a lot of money to go to Iowa by train, but there wouldn't be time to drive. How much school would everyone have to miss if we went? Who would take Mother's classes? Nothing could be decided until we had more information. Uncle Dean had said he'd call tomorrow once plans were made; Uncle Dean and Aunt Velma (Papa's youngest sister) were the only ones living near Grandpa and Grandma Weaver.

Even after Grandpa and Grandma left, Mother continued to shiver. "Kathie, will you sleep with me tonight?" she asked. "I simply can't stop shivering." Sleeping with Mother was usually a treat reserved for the night before our birthday. This night I crawled into bed with her, not to hear a story about my birth, but to lie against her, to be there so she wouldn't be alone.

When I got home from school the next day, Grandma was there ironing. Supper was cooking on the stove. Everything felt surreal. I laid down my school books and took over ironing my blouses, hurrying to finish and then help pack suitcases. Uncle Dean had called with funeral information earlier in the day. He had urged Mother to bring all three of us, saying that he and Aunt Velma would pay for our tickets. We needed to leave that evening. Papa's cousin Elwood, who was also going, would drive us to Staunton, where we would meet additional relatives, all going on the train to Iowa.

In spite of myself, I felt excited. We were going on a train, leaving behind the routines of school and homework. Even my weight of sadness couldn't completely blot out this anticipation. Meeting others at the station and all boarding the train together distracted me. Trying to sleep sitting up didn't work well. I kept going over and over in my mind the fact that I would never see Grandpa and Grandma Weaver again.

The next morning in Cincinnati, the train stopped long enough for us to have breakfast in the station. After a night of fitful sleep, I sat at a counter in a haze of cigarette smoke and amid the din of many voices, clinking plates, and crackly announcements. The bitter coffee Mother let me order woke me up. My crisp French toast, so saturated with oil that it seemed to be deep-fried, had sweet syrup dripping down its sides. The bustling station was charged with the energy of people traveling. No one paid any attention to me. I didn't stand out as different. Grandpa and Grandma's deaths felt a world away, and for the moment I was part of a big, exciting crowd.

Arriving in Iowa City and then at Grandpa Weaver's empty house brought me back sharply into my own world. We would stay there with cousins, uncles, and aunts, sleeping in beds freshly made by Grandma Weaver before they left for the wedding. She wanted to be ready in case wedding guests stopped overnight on their way home. But nothing was the same. This place that had always made me happy felt empty, even though every bed was full. Its heart had stopped beating. Loss appeared at every turn—no loaves of Grandma's fresh bread cooling on the cook stove, no Grandpa tinkering in his shed, none of the usual happy joking among family members.

After the funeral the next day, we stood and watched as the two coffins were slowly lowered into the ground. I stood next to Kris, the cousin closest my age. Mother, who stood with all the aunts and their spouses, suddenly let out a sharp cry. It sounded wordless to me, but later Jeanie said she had cried out "Melvin!" My cousin Elwood, a few years older than me, quickly stepped to her side and put his arm around her. I watched, feeling both relieved that someone was there to stand with Mother and guilty that it hadn't been me.

The next day, the family emptied Grandma's china cupboard and took down pictures from the walls, leaving unfaded spots in the wallpaper. We then began to divide household items. I walked around the long dining room table, which held all of Grandma's pretty dishes. Each grandchild could choose one thing. I circled several times before I settled on a glass pitcher and goblet set that my aunts said had been a wedding gift. I traced the flower pattern with my finger trying to imagine Grandma as a bride, wondering what she had looked like, how she had felt? Then I looked at the room, already half empty, and grief filled my chest. I wanted to return everything to its usual place and see Grandma standing there with her quiet smile and a toothpick in the corner of her mouth. This had all been too sudden. We had not said goodbye to her or Grandpa, nor had we been given any time to get used to the idea of them being gone.

On the trip home, nothing felt right. The departing train arrived late. It was dirty and the seats sagged. My throat was sore and my nose started to run—a cold was coming on. Exhaustion set in from deep emotions and nights of little sleep. I stared out the window. The last several days seemed a dream that flitted from one scene to another in a disordered jumble: The aunts talking about how good it was that Grandpa and Grandma could go together, having experienced the loss of four of their eight children. Seeing Grandma's body in the casket, her veined hands folded across her middle. Family worship in the living room when Uncle Leroy read about Saul and Jonathan in the Bible, how they were not parted in death. Laughter around the edges of the grief. My school work waiting at home. Mother's cry at the cemetery.

All this and more ran through my mind. I sat in a semi-stupor and mostly endured the long train ride back to ordinary life. My classmates would be the same. They would have no idea of my new reality, which felt more real than school. It would be hard to go back to being the schoolgirl I was just days ago. Life had changed once more and would never be quite the same.

We got home late Saturday night. The next morning, we all slept late, and none of us went to church.

Our black 1951 Chevy drove north on Route 11 between green fields and white fences. This had been the last day of school for the year, the best day as far as I was concerned. Even Carol, who hated to be seen in our old car, was happy. We were driving to MD's Chicken in the Rough restaurant in New Market, Mother's annual end-of-the-school-year treat to us. It was the only time we ate out, except when we traveled. Chicken in the Rough, as the name suggests, was not a fancy place. Its main menu item was a fried half of a chicken served with a soft white roll and honey. Along with that came a salad of iceberg lettuce, carrot, and cucumber slices with Thousand Island dressing and one large pimento-stuffed green olive as garnish. We never had Thousand Island dressing at home and rarely olives. Grandma and Mother's cooking was not Southern enough to include fried chicken. Neither did we ever eat "in the rough," which meant being given no utensils and eating the chicken with our fingers. Everything about this meal was novel. I had been looking forward to it for weeks. My mouth began to water for the crisp, salty chicken and the soft roll and sweet honey, and we weren't even there yet.

Finally, we arrived and were seated. A waitress brought our salads, and I took off the olive to save for the end. Then came the chicken, as delicious as ever. We ate slowly, wanting to make the meal last. I could never finish my chicken half, nor could anyone else. We would take some home, although it was never as crispy the second time. I sighed with satisfaction as I cleaned my greasy fingers in my finger bowl, which was actually a tiny tin bucket. I wished the meal weren't over—it went far too quickly. I'd have to wait a whole year to have this meal again. As we drove home, I looked out at the same fields we had passed earlier. Now long shadows from the trees inched across them, and the setting sun briefly turned grass to gold before it faded to dark green. The Massanutten Mountain stood, immovable in space but gradually shifting from blue to purple as the light seeped away. Moist, warm air blew through our open windows, carrying with it the sweet smell of fresh-cut grass and honeysuckle. The school year was complete—no more tests or papers. When we got home, we could sit in the backyard to watch fireflies' neon flashes as they rose higher and higher. When I went to bed, I could take a book with me to read before I turned out the lamp.

Summer stretched before me. We would travel to Pennsylvania to visit relatives. We'd have some of the best food of the year: watermelon, fresh peas, corn on the cob, thick slices of tomatoes still warm from the sun, and fuzzy-skinned peaches. We'd have work too, like shelling peas as we sat in the shade of our locust tree, husking corn gingerly so as not to touch worms who might have eaten their way into the ear, canning peaches and tomatoes in the hot, steamy kitchen. And some warm afternoon I'd walk into Grandma's kitchen and breathe in the nose-tingling smell of the cinnamon and clove oils she used for pickling watermelon rind—my only job had been to help eat slices of crisp watermelon so the rind could be pickled. Nights would bring welcome cool breezes after the day's heat, and through the open window, I'd hear the tenor-toned bell from the School ring 10 o'clock as I turned one more page and then another in my book. As far as I was concerned, summer could last forever.

Part II

A Boat to Carry Me

I opened the blinds a crack like eyelids, and it all came
exploding in on me . . . oh yes, the world.

—ANNIE DILLARD, *THE WRITING LIFE*

22

Wanting More

I WAS BACK ON the campus of the School, this time as a college student. Once again I felt numb, sleepwalking through freshman orientation and my first weeks of classes. Like high school, I knew my way around; I knew the teachers, and the classrooms were all familiar. I didn't doubt that I could do the work, but I felt strangely out of place. My group of high school friends provided familiarity, but most of this new class were strangers. Many of them seemed confident and more comfortable than me, even though I'd grown up in this place. As I sat in class or walked to chapel or had lunch in the cafeteria, I listened to others' happy chatter and observed the easy way they seemed to inhabit this space. I wondered at their willingness to volunteer for extracurricular activities or to run for various leadership positions. I couldn't imagine myself doing any of those things.

College had been the obvious next step to take and Eastern Mennonite College the only school I considered. I didn't expect a lot other than hard work sprinkled with good times among friends. I found my elementary education classes boring and was intimidated by my mostly male classmates in history classes, history being my second major. During my first and second years, many days were shrouded in gray, and I often dragged through them feeling as if I were wearing a backpack filled with rocks.

In my third year, Carol transferred to Indiana University to earn a piano performance degree. I thought she was brave to go far from home to a big campus where she knew no one. I wasn't sure I'd have the courage to do the same. Nevertheless, when her letters came, filled with tales of

new experiences and unique people, I chafed at my familiar surroundings. I wrote to her:

> I'm getting more and more restless . . . I feel like I have to go away
> for a while and be me. Not that I have great restrictions but that
> I'm so hemmed in at every turn. I just can't get away from family
> . . . [Grandma who is] "dreadfully worried" about K.S. and me
> going to D.C., or [Aunt Esther who] stops in to tell me how I did
> on a test I would as soon not discuss personally with the teacher,
> or [Jeanie who] has done the breakfast dishes so can't possibly
> help at supper . . . I do feel that I'm needed here at home this year,
> but sometimes it would be nice to be on my own.

Even so, the outside world inched closer and sometimes seeped in.
We saw on television the horrors of the Vietnam War far away, but then
a young woman whose husband was fighting there moved in across the
street for summer school, and I saw firsthand how that horror played out
in one person's life. She and I sometimes walked to the campus together,
and she talked about shutting out all news because it was too terrifying to
hear it. She seemed like a fragile shell of a person, simply going through
the motions without really living.

One warm spring evening as I was studying in the library, someone
came in to tell us that Martin Luther King Jr. had just been assassinated.
I stared at her, almost unbelieving, even though we all had known this
might happen, given the resistance he faced. I immediately headed to
Grandpa's house to watch television, knowing riots were likely to break
out right away. Chapel the next day felt almost like a funeral. We were
all shaken. We *were* part of this country, even though as Mennonites we
traditionally stayed out of politics. This tragedy touched us all.

I spent an exciting study weekend in D.C. learning about city life. On
Friday night, we walked the crowded streets of the Georgetown neighborhood, and I felt exhilarated to be part of that vibrant, diverse place.
We went to the Savile Book Shop, which I had heard advertised on the
radio throughout my childhood. It had been part of another world that
I never imagined I would inhabit, and now I wandered from room to
room, almost dazed to be in it. I could hardly wait to tell the family.

My restlessness was fed by such experiences. A dazzling world danced invitingly just beyond the places I felt safe. After that weekend, I wrote to Carol:

> There is so much I want to read and do that I am completely overwhelmed. Things seem to come at me from all directions tonight. Sometimes I would like to be terribly worldly and sophisticated—to study history and the arts, live in some big impersonal place like NYC where I wouldn't need to be responsible to anyone and where I would have many good things to do. Then I feel ashamed and guilty that I am so unconcerned about anyone else and all the sadness and suffering in the world . . . I'm afraid that in order to avoid really facing either extreme I'll be willing to settle down to some namby-pamby, soft mealy life that won't offer much but progressive inertia.

I felt my restlessness intensely but had no idea how to move beyond it. I couldn't envision a future that would satisfy me and be realistic at the same time.

23

Stirrings of Change

My senior year had a flavor all its own. The four years that had loomed like an eternity before me were nearly over, and I was relieved to be getting close to the end. But a more immediate change presented itself, something I had never imagined would happen. I moved into the dorm.

Mother had a sabbatical year and made plans to spend it in post-graduate work at Indiana University, where she and Carol could live together. Carol wasn't sure how she liked that arrangement, but I was ecstatic. Jeanie, who was ready for her freshman year of college at EMC, would also be in a dorm, even though she would have preferred living at home. For once, I was little concerned with my sisters' feelings and began to make plans to room with Donna Carol, my best friend from high school. The opportunity was too good to be true.

Perhaps it was the first blush of euphoria before dorm life; perhaps it was my restless desire for change. Whichever it was, I got my hair cut short just weeks before school started—short enough to wear in a flip. The church taught that women were to have long hair. Although Grandpa was disappointed, he told me so only once, saying he wouldn't talk about it again. I think he knew he couldn't hold back change.

The new style required skills I had never learned. I knew how to braid my hair or roll it into a bun or French twist, but I didn't know how to use curlers or hair spray. My first attempts did not produce good results, so a friend came to help. I was staying at Grandpa's house—Mother had already left for Indiana—and I found myself learning these new skills as I sat on the same kitchen stool I'd sat on when Grandma braided my hair. I watched in the mirror as my friend Liz rolled my hair, one strand at a time, around fat pink rollers, fastening each with a long bobby pin. The rollers and pins felt like little hedgehogs prickling my scalp and looked like small culverts lining my head. In spite of that process, I found short hair freeing. I told Donna Carol that the best thing about loose hair was feeling the wind blow through it, and she responded by calling me a hopeless romantic.

After a Sunday dinner at Grandpa and Grandma's house. The wind was blowing my hair as I posed with my roommate Donna Carol, Carol (my sister), and good friend Margaret *(left to right)*.

Donna Carol and I moved into a dorm that had just been completed. I was excited as I unpacked my things in a fresh room, still smelling of cut wood, new carpet, and paint. I set up my stereo set, organized books on the shelf above my new desk, and filled my drawers. Our room had a built-in washbowl between the two wardrobe units, and that felt luxurious. I put a rug from home in front of the washbowl and hung my favorite Vermeer print on the wall, and the room felt complete.

For the first time, I was living away from home. I was free—on my own in a way that was entirely new. I inhabited the best of both worlds. I wasn't responsible for any household chores, I was not answerable to Mother in any daily way, and I could be involved in college student life more completely. At the same time, our house was only two blocks away, and when I dropped by to get a book or forgotten garment, the renters would offer me a cup of tea. I could also go two blocks in the other direction to Grandpa's house whenever I wished. Some days I'd go there for lunch, just to spend time with Grandpa and Grandma, but mostly I reveled in being truly part of the college.

My letters to Mother and Carol were full of dorm happenings, like going to a friend's room to help her with knitting or conversing with late-night visitors—all of us in our pajamas, fixing tea and peanut butter crackers in the small kitchen next to the lounge. I wrote to Mother that I was afraid I was spending so much time socializing that I wouldn't get assignments done on time. I was happier than I had ever been before in college.

At the end of my junior year, I had written to Carol saying that I had achieved an unbroken record for the year: no dates. That too was about to change. One Friday evening in October, I went alone to the chapel for a lecture about the Middle East that was given by a visiting scholar. Afterward, I paused on the porch to talk with someone and noticed Wayne Kurtz standing off to the side. He seemed to be waiting for someone, and I wondered vaguely if it was me, but Aunt Esther and Elsie (her first cousin, who also taught in the Education Department) came up just then. They were heading across the campus in the same direction as I was, so we set out together, the two of them flanking me like guards. Halfway across campus, we parted ways. As I proceeded toward my dorm, I heard someone call out. At first, I wasn't sure it was me who was being called, but then I turned around and saw Wayne a little distance behind me.

Wayne had graduated from college the year before and I knew him casually. Now he was working in the community. During the summer we had both sung in an informal chamber group, and Carol, home for the summer from Indiana University, had accompanied us. I had been dismayed when Wayne asked her for a date, but not because I wanted to date him. It seemed that all Carol had to do was come home and, voilà, she had a date. She wasn't really interested in him, so we schemed to get him connected with a cousin of ours. That went nowhere. The last time I had seen him was at the water fountain under the big clock in the Ad Building, shortly before school started. I was at my work study job in the registrar's office and had come out into the hall to get a drink. Wayne happened to be passing by, and we talked briefly. I had thought no more of it.

Now, here he was, asking me to go to the Bard's Nest, the college coffee house, for a cup of tea. We sat and sipped tea as someone strummed a guitar and sang. Wayne asked me to join him the following evening for an all-school "county fair" event in the gym, and I agreed.

When I got back to the dorm, I told Donna Carol and our next-door neighbors who all made a big deal of it. I felt ambivalent, but at least it was a date. The next evening, they all hovered as I got ready to go, teasing me and giving all sorts of silly advice.

Another date followed and then another. My ambivalence continued. He wasn't the intellectual I imagined marrying, but I felt comfortable with him. He was kind, attentive, and helpful, solid and dependable. One evening we sat in the college snack shop and he talked about his concern for his younger brothers, whom he hoped would not need to struggle the way he had to get away from home and find the freedom they wanted. I was impressed by his level of caring.

On another evening we went to a coffeehouse in Harrisonburg. Because it was so crowded, we were seated at a table with another young man who happened to be from Wayne's home congregation. While I ate my cherry cheesecake, they talked about people I didn't know, but then the conversation turned to the two years Wayne had spent in Greece. He talked about the travel he had done in Europe and the Middle East and his interest in going overseas again. Compared to our tablemate and many of my classmates, he seemed older and more worldly-wise.

Even so, I continued to be unsure of my feelings. After he took me to visit his family in Pennsylvania and I met his siblings, I came home even more uncertain. I feared that he would expect me to stay at home and not work, like his sisters-in-law. I had no grand career plans, but I didn't want to feel hemmed in. Wayne blithely assured me that he wanted me to be free to do what I wanted.

As the weeks went by, my ambivalence slowly faded. We shared interests in music, art, and travel. He was competent and well-respected at his work, and he was a good cook. But more than that, I could be myself with him and feel at ease. He enthusiastically affirmed me and was willing to do almost anything to help me, including typing term papers. He wasn't the knight in shining armor that Donna Carol and I joked about coming to rescue us when we wanted to avoid dealing with some unpleasant circumstance, but his kind brown eyes drew me in and held me. Besides, who would want to keep a knight's armor shiny and well-oiled all the time? I didn't want that kind of relationship.

We became engaged in April and decided on a December wedding, which would come during my Christmas break from teaching. We didn't want to wait a whole year to get married.

24

Teacher and Bride

MARJORIE GUENGERICH'S LITTLE GRAY VW Beetle pulled up in front of Mother's house. I went out the front door, books and papers in hand, and climbed in. As we wound our way through the back streets of Harrisonburg, trying to avoid as many traffic lights as possible, I tried to assess my feelings. It was 1969, and I was heading into my first day as a "real" teacher. How would it go? Did I know enough to handle a group of lively fourth graders?

We reached Route 33 and drove east toward Massanutten Peak, which loomed larger and larger as we approached, the blue of its folds slowly coming into focus as distinct green trees and gray outcroppings of rock. It was a reassuring sign, I thought, that this mountain—above which the sun had appeared each morning for most of my life—would be right beside me here at school, almost close enough to touch.

We turned into the McGaheysville Elementary School parking lot and entered the nearly new building. Marjorie turned off at the first door on the left for her first-grade classroom, and I continued on down the hall, past the third-grade rooms to mine. It was as neat and quiet as I had left it the day before. I paused for one moment, surveying the orderly room, and then went in and laid down my books on the desk. There were no yellow buses yet, and the halls were empty except for teachers hurriedly finishing up last-minute tasks. I stood in the quiet, gathering my courage. Before long, buses began to arrive. The halls filled with noisy, eager children, some of whom spilled into my room. They looked at me curiously and I watched them with equal interest. We would be spending thirty hours a week together for the next nine months, and we had never met before.

More students came with each bus arrival, and the peaceful quiet of my room was shattered by chattering voices. The harsh buzz of the electronic bell sounded and all eyes turned toward me. "Good morning," I said. "I am Miss Weaver, and I will be your teacher this year. For right now, sit in any desk you want. We'll figure out seating later." More chatter ensued along with directives and disagreements as friends tried to negotiate seats close to each other. When everyone was seated, I proceeded with a roll call. "I might not remember your names right away," I told them, "but I hope I will know them all very soon." The children quieted down a little, but not as much as I hoped, and now I had no supervising teacher to step in to establish order.

I got through the first day—and the second. I again felt like a sleepwalker, numbly making my way through a layer of haze. By the time I got home each evening, I barely remembered what had happened that day. This was just the beginning of the year, I told myself. Things would get better. Several weeks later I wrote to Carol, "School was terribly noisy today. I don't know how I'll ever quiet them down, but I'll keep working at it." I had assumed the beginning would be difficult, but things weren't getting better. I tried to figure out ways to teach my lively students that would catch and hold their attention, but the classroom remained too noisy and chaotic for my comfort.

Parts of teaching I enjoyed. In November I wrote to Carol:

> One of my poorest little boys brought me a clay pot that he had made all by himself from clay in his driveway. About a week before we had had a television art lesson on pottery. He had made it of coils and smoothed it with a stick like they did [in the art lesson] . . . The clay seemed very good. It didn't crumble or crack at all. Now I have a whole dishpan of clay at school waiting for 350 eager little fingers (and thumbs). We won't be able to fire what we make, but at least the children will have the opportunity to make something.

I was touched by the diligence and initiative my student had shown because he was challenged academically and never shone in other classes. For once he could be in the spotlight. I also enjoyed the idea of such activities, although the mess and confusion made me anxious.

❦

As December approached, I spent more time in wedding-related activities, and my concerns about teaching moved to the background. When vacation began, I put school completely out of my mind for two weeks and basked in the excitement of my "real" life.

Our wedding went well, except that most of Wayne's family from Pennsylvania didn't make it. I was about to head for my planned bubble bath when Mother called me to the phone. It was Wayne's sister-in-law saying they were at home. They had had to turn around because of a jackknifed trailer truck and snow from the previous day drifting around it. Wayne's brother, the best man, would not be there, and what was more, they didn't know whether his parents had gotten through before the accident or were heading back home as well.

I called Wayne and we tried to figure out what to do. We needed to find a replacement for his best man before the tuxedo rental place closed for the day. Wayne could think of no one nearby to press into service, so I asked a casual friend who was dating one of my bridesmaids, and he consented. There were other helper slots I needed to fill with substitutes, necessitating more calls. Finally, around four o'clock, Wayne's mother called to say they were home too. I could hear the tears in her voice, and I felt sorry for her, but by then I was focused on my own preparation. The imagined bubble bath morphed into a quick splash in the tub. Then it was time to go. I sent the white velvet dress I had sewed so carefully with Mother, who drove her car to the church, but I pulled on new high boots, put on my new blue coat, and walked the few blocks to Park View Mennonite Church, where the wedding would take place.

I was too happy to spend time regretting that some couldn't be there. Disappointment would come later, but I wanted nothing to mar the joy of this event. I wanted to go through it fully present and aware of each moment. As I stood on Uncle Bob's arm, waiting to begin my walk down the aisle, he commented that this was an important moment in my life, and I interrupted him, saying, "Uncle Bob, stop, or you'll make me cry." Then the music started and we began walking toward Wayne, who was waiting for me.

After the reception in the church basement, Wayne and I left cold and snowy Harrisonburg for a honeymoon in Williamsburg, where the temperatures hovered in the sixties all the following week. When we returned home to our new apartment, just a block away from Mother's house, I wrote to Carol saying that I felt "more deeply satisfied, happy, peaceful, and fulfilled" than I ever had before.

Wayne and me on our wedding day.

Returning to teaching was a completely different matter. It felt like an abrupt re-entry into a world I would rather have left behind—along with my unmarried state. I tried to convince myself that I liked it, that I just needed to figure out how to do it better. But every Sunday afternoon I began wandering around our small apartment feeling restless and unable to focus on anything. By evening I had worked up a full-blown bad mood. The school week was coming. How would I deal with Gary when he started clowning around during math class? What if Wendy wouldn't stay in her desk? I still had to come up with a new bulletin board, and I needed to record spelling scores. Friday, like every Friday, had been chaotic. How could I get a handle on quieting my class? Faye, my fellow fourth-grade teacher, seemed to have the knack. I wondered why I didn't. What was wrong with me? I complained to Wayne. I was grumpy—no, I didn't want ice cream, no, I didn't want to play a game. Everything seemed overwhelming, impossible. I wished it were Friday or, even better, June.

I also went from one cold to another. Faye asked me one day if this was a new cold or still the old one. I was embarrassed because I knew there was a connection between my constant colds and my intense unhappiness. I didn't know how to change that. I assumed my teaching problems were due to my deficiencies.

My summer break was glorious. I stayed at home, read, sewed some new dresses, made iced tea to share with a neighbor, and had supper ready when Wayne got home from work. At the end of August, I cried, not wanting to return to school. I felt trapped. Once school began, I wrote to Carol:

> I'm in one of my Sunday night bad moods. I want to do something wild and accept no work or responsibility for tomorrow. In fact, what would make me happy would be to stay home . . . Why am I such a retreatist? It seems that any work or responsibility frightens me. Is it pure laziness or do I have some other hidden problems?

Then again in November, I confided to her:

> About losing myself in school, I think my biggest problem is with my own personality. It's hard for me to relax with the children and accept them as they are. I'm defensive and a little scared, I think, and therefore tend to be rigid and uncompromising . . . It really distresses me. One can spend every waking moment on school things, but if one can't carry them out with patience, good humor, and everything else, it's impossible to get anywhere. I try to work at it, but when I think about it . . . I feel so inadequate and inferior that I don't want to go to school ever again. I guess I don't have enough spunk, but it's awfully hard to work on changing one's basic reaction. You know I'm not much good at covering my real feelings. It seems that I'm everything I don't want to be and nothing that I do want to be.

I felt miserable and put myself down, but never did I ask if I had chosen the wrong job. I was sure the problem was my lack of skill. I identified with one of my colleagues who, after a difficult week of teaching, declared, "I'm going home and getting seven months pregnant this weekend!"

But instead of getting pregnant, I went to Africa.

25

Botswana

WE WERE OFF ON the first real adventure of our married life—off to Africa. When we called Wayne's parents from the airport for our final goodbye, Wayne's mother was teary. As we waited with Mother for our flight to be called, she cried and cried, but I had no tears. I was about to have my first airplane ride, and I was not disappointed. Everything about it was fascinating: the takeoff, the view from the window as Washington, D.C. shrank to dollhouse size and smaller and then was left behind for glimpses of coastline and ocean. I liked the peanuts and Coke served by the stewardess (as they were then called) and the nifty fold-out tray to hold them.

Wayne and I had signed up for a three-year term in Botswana, a country so new it wasn't yet on most maps. My assignment was to teach in a primary school, and Wayne's was to do accounting for a group of small technical training schools, called Brigades, that were scattered around the country.

We were going to Africa in the way I had always imagined—with Mennonite Central Committee (MCC). Mother's first secretarial job in the 1940s had been at its headquarters in Pennsylvania. Peter Dyck, the almost-famous person from my childhood, had worked for MCC, and so had Wayne during the years he was in Greece. MCC had been a household name all my life. Now it was my turn to be a part of it.

The most difficult aspect of leaving home was being away for three years. I had never been gone that long, and there would be no weekend trips back to see family or to pick up things I had forgotten. MCC gave us a list of items to take along that might be unavailable or prohibitively expensive: good underwear, flannel pajamas (it could be cold in the winter), king-size sheets for combining two twin beds into one, plastic containers with lids (Tupperware). One friend suggested that we make tape recordings of some of our favorite records, and another suggested that it would be helpful to take a few small items that felt like home. Wayne recorded a Harry Belafonte and Miriam Makeba record and some Christmas music on cassette tapes, and I chose our favorite placemat and napkin set and the afghan I was in the process of knitting. We packed and repacked, trying to decide exactly what to take and what to leave. I made room for my favorite cookbook, and we took chocolate chips.

I decided not to take any coverings. By college I had worn one less and less often—mostly for chapel and church. Now I would be going into a culture where they were completely unknown, and I saw no reason to take one. I knew this was a practice I was leaving behind for good.

On our way to Botswana, we spent ten days in Greece seeing where Wayne had lived and meeting some of his old friends. Then we flew via South Africa to Gaborone, the newly built capital city of Botswana. As we approached in our small plane, I looked down on vast stretches of barren ground tumbled with rocks and punctuated by stunted thorn trees. When the town came into view, it looked more like a large village than a city. From the air I could see the carefully laid-out grid of streets, and I remembered reading that wild animals had roamed there not many years before.

We descended into a cool, cloudy day. I had pictured a hot place, but instead I found myself digging in a suitcase for a sweater. We would spend our first days at Joan and Bertha's house, known jokingly as the MCC Hilton because they hosted most new MCC volunteers when they arrived in the country. For lunch we had familiar peanut butter sandwiches in a warmish kitchen, but afterward I dug my jacket out of the bottom of a suitcase. I couldn't stop shivering. Our bedroom was damp and cold, but at least with its single bed, Wayne and I could snuggle close enough to keep warm at night.

Before many days passed, the sun shone and we explored the town. Gaborone had a library, a hospital, a bookstore, a bank, several large churches, a small collection of shops, and, of course, government office buildings, none more than two or three stories high. The town contained most of the twenty miles of paved roads in the country. Everywhere I went I felt vibrancy and excitement, an almost palpable sense of possibility and pride in this new town and new country.

Within a week or two, we settled into a small temporary flat. I began teaching at Thornhill Primary School, where both Joan and Bertha taught, and Wayne started to travel for his job. It was then that I became homesick. While I was at school, I was fine, but when I returned to our empty flat, the distance from everyone I knew felt immense and as good as permanent. Sometimes a letter from home greeted me, but Mother's letters, typed on crinkly onionskin paper, could not carry with them her presence, and I felt even more lonely after reading them. Neither could my slim blue aerograms carry in their neat folds the weight of the sand, the heat of the sun, or my longing to be home. Our three-year assignment stretched endlessly ahead of me—I couldn't even think that far. I ate my solitary bowl of cold cereal and listened to the perpetual call of Cape mourning doves. They sounded as sad as I felt.

The school day started early and finished at one o'clock, so I had afternoons free. I would venture from the cool, dim interior of our flat into the hot sun and walk several blocks to the Botswana National Museum and the public library, where I could check out books. Sometimes I explored the shops on the mall, tilting my sandals as I walked so the sand would fall out with each step. I bought freshly butchered mince (hamburger) at the butcher shop and teaching supplies at Botswana Book Centre. I pored over baskets, bracelets, and brightly dyed fabric at Botswanacraft. To my amazement, I found Colgate toothpaste at the chemist's and Kellogg's cornflakes at the small grocery shop. One night I went to the cinema alone to see *Alice's Restaurant*, and for two brief hours, I felt like I was back at home again.

Living in Gaborone meant that we frequently saw other volunteers, both from MCC and other organizations, who came to the city on business or for shopping. We learned to know each other quickly. It was not unusual to have someone drop in to visit and stay for a meal, nor was it unusual to have a friend—or a friend of a friend—stay overnight. The rule of hospitality was that you offered whatever you had with no apologies. No one expected a fancy meal, and a bed on the floor was adequate.

Thornhill was the only elementary school in Gaborone for English-speaking students. The children of high-ranking government officials attended it, as did embassy children. Teaching there brought a set of challenges different than the ones I had faced at home. Resources were minimal. Even though I taught the most privileged children in the country, we had no library, no encyclopedias, no film projectors or television, and few, if any, art supplies. The British headmaster assumed more authority than principals in the US were given. I needed to learn African history to teach my class. And my vocabulary changed: I taught *maths*, told the children to form a *queue straightaway*, and reminded them about *full stops* at the end of sentences. I cut paper on the *guillotine*.

The cultural diversity of my class more than made up for the lack of materials. My bright, articulate students had awareness of the larger world that my McGaheysville students had lacked. Discipline issues were far fewer, enabling me to relax and enjoy my class. Teachers came from diverse backgrounds as well, and I enjoyed learning to know them. Many were British, but there were a few Canadians and Batswana (members of the Tswana people). Midmorning, we gathered for a tea break, and I drank sweet, milky tea along with a *biscuit* and enjoyed the soft clinking of spoons against china tea cups. It felt like a civilized custom—one I looked forward to each day.

When Wayne was home from his travels, life felt more normal. After occupying two temporary living places, we were finally assigned a flat not far from Thornhill, and we eagerly began to turn it into our home. I bought secondhand drapes from volunteers who were leaving. Wayne built a speaker cabinet, and to make it look like our speakers at home, I covered the sides with burlap. Above it we hung a Java print with an elaborate gold-and-maroon medallion pattern. We created a lamp from a painted tin can and bought a large sisal rug to cover the cement floor.

This mixture of secondhand, burlap-covered, painted creations may have looked like what it was by daylight, but one night I dreamed that I entered the room and found it hushed by soft carpet and plush sofas. Velvet replaced the corduroy curtains, and everything was more vibrantly colored than in reality. I marveled in the dream at the beauty of what we had created.

It was early January of 1973. The rushing water of Victoria Falls created a background rumble. We found a grassy place beyond the falls' spray to sit and watch the water's continuous flow as we thought of what was coming soon. We were about to move. We had lived in Gaborone since we came to Botswana a year and a half ago. Now we were relocating to Ramotswa, a traditional village and center of the Bamalete tribe, twenty miles south of Gaborone on the South African border. There Wayne would work as the secretary (administrator) of the Bamalete Lutheran Hospital run by a German Lutheran mission, and I would teach at Mokgosi III Memorial School. We were happy that Wayne would no longer need to travel, but I was sad to be leaving Thornhill and Gaborone.

Our conversation turned to a question we had debated before: should we try to have a baby now? I leaned toward waiting until we went back to the States. Wayne, who had just turned 30, wanted to try right away. We went back and forth, listing the pros and cons of each option. If we waited until it was convenient, we would never have a baby, Wayne declared, although he acknowledged that having a child would impact me more since I would be the one to stop work and provide primary care. We finally decided to try, and I began to feel excited in spite of my earlier reservations.

In the meantime, the upcoming move claimed our attention, though it was a simple process: all we needed to take were personal items, kitchen utensils, and the few pieces of furniture we had built. It all fit easily on the back of our small Toyota pickup.

I fell in love with the new house in Ramotswa even before we moved in. I learned that it had been the original hospital, a small square building of four rooms, attached to another small cottage that housed some of the nurses. Once again, we set about making it ours. We hung the corduroy curtains, put up our few pictures and the Java print, and arranged our meager library on a bookshelf along with our growing collection of pottery and baskets. I had no dream of splendor, but we had a cozy house.

Perhaps my favorite part of the house was the front porch, shaded by large trees, where I often sat in the late afternoon to read. From there I looked out over the prickly pears and leggy poinsettias in our small garden to the big century-old Lutheran church, complete with flying buttresses, looking as if it had been transported right out of some European town. I often heard the choir practicing there—sometimes familiar songs, sometimes not. Just beyond it was the hospital. Patients and family members walked around outside in the warm afternoon air. The lattice along the front of the porch created diamonds of sun on the floor, and birds sang. Far off in the village, people called to each other, dogs barked, goats bleated, children played. Some days the aroma of beer bread baking floated down from the village bakery, and I would make the short walk to buy a loaf or two, hoping it would still be warm when we ate our evening meal.

At night the only sounds were occasional dogs barking, distant drum-beating, sometimes singing, and the on-off hum of the generator at the South African border station just beyond our house. The sky was filled with more stars than I had ever seen. I learned to identify the Southern Cross but not a lot more. The quiet and peace of night settled in around me.

Ramotswa was a traditional village of round, mud-plastered, thatch-roofed huts called *rondovals*. Families usually had several huts clustered within a fence or walled *lapa* (compound). One hut might be for cooking, another for grain storage, and others for sleeping. Some houses, like ours, were constructed with cement blocks and tin roofs.

Even here we found ourselves in a mix of cultures. Our neighbors on the church-hospital compound were German, Dutch, South African, Canadian, and British, along with interns from Ireland and the US. The nurses in the other half of our house were Batswana. In contrast, my fellow teachers were all Batswana except for the other standard (grade) six teacher, Mr. Semuli, who was a political refugee from Lesotho. I came to know him and his wife quite well because we were all outsiders at the school. They—along with Agatha, a single teacher from another part of Botswana—visited us frequently and we visited them. I felt rich in friendships.

On my first day of school, I followed meandering footpaths through the village, past courtyards where women swept the bare ground and smoke from breakfast fires hung in the air. I could hear children's voices even before the school came into view. Then I saw Mokgosi III Memorial Primary School ahead of me, four single-story buildings arranged to form an interior courtyard. I walked in at a corner between buildings. Each classroom door opened directly onto the courtyard, and a stand pipe and faucet stood to one side of the open space—the only water source for the entire school. Children were running and playing in this dusty square or clustering in small groups talking. Into this cacophony came the ringing of a handbell and the swirling mass of children "sorted themselves out" into orderly queues by class, each standing next to their teacher. After announcements in Setswana and English the children sang in Setswana a song I knew in English as "Beside Thy Cradle Here I Stand." To them it was just a hymn from the big church next to the hospital. To me it was a chorale from Bach's Christmas Oratorio, and the familiar melody reassured me as I faced this new venture. I smiled to myself. The German Lutheran missionaries had clearly left their mark here.

The front porch of our Ramotswa house, where I spent many late afternoons reading and listening to the choir practice.

But following my students into our classroom wrenched me back into unfamiliar territory. Everything felt dusty, even though I had tried to clean the day before. My forty-seven students found their places, two at each double desk, except for one desk where three crowded together. The blackboard was rough and its paint chipping at places. A single dingy bulletin board and well-worn paperback textbooks stored in a small cupboard were the only resources at hand. Speaking slowly and carefully, I greeted the class and made my way through a roll call of mostly unfamiliar names I wasn't sure how to pronounce. The morning stretched endlessly before me. I began with reading class, passing out the paperback readers. When I asked students to read aloud, some read proficiently, some haltingly, and others not at all. We progressed to maths, which evidenced the same range of ability, and then it was recess time. With a quiet sigh of relief, I said, "You may put your books away for recess." Everyone stared at me blankly. "Put your books in your desks," I enunciated more slowly and carefully. Still blank faces. I walked to a student's desk, took the maths book and, reaching around, placed it on the shelf under the desk. *Uh hays* (exclamation of recognition) broke out as comprehension dawned and then laughter. I didn't have to demonstrate "You may go outside."

After the children left, I stood alone for a moment in the quiet room, wanting to go back to my peaceful front porch. This job seemed impossible. I didn't want to do it. But I went outside to watch the children play and stumbled on through the day. Finally, 1:30 came, and the dismissal bell rang. Several girls swept the floor with short hand brooms, raising as much dust as they swept away. I gathered my books and glanced around the drab, gritty room, relieved to be going home, away from all this— home where I could be at peace. But that was not to be.

As I walked out, Mr. Semuli, my next-door colleague said, "I'll see you this afternoon."

"This afternoon?" I asked, puzzled.

"For study time," he replied.

"Study time?" I asked incredulously.

"Yes," he replied, equally puzzled by my response. "The students need time to study, so they return every afternoon."

"No one told me about this," I said, trying not to sound angry. "We didn't do that in Gaborone."

Mr. Semuli shrugged as if to suggest that those privileged students lived in another world.

"This is what we do here," he replied with finality.

Once again school became a challenge, zapping most of my excitement about our new surroundings. I did what I could to make it better. I talked with the headmaster and worked out an arrangement to come in only two afternoons rather than four, an arrangement my students didn't object to. I figured that I could teach them what they needed to know within regular school hours. I brought in a bright yellow bookshelf Wayne had built for our Gaborone kitchen to use for the set of World Book encyclopedias I had gotten free through the US Consulate. Wayne built another bulletin board, and we painted both frames green. I didn't consider how other teachers might view my improvements. Mr. Semuli was bold enough to ask me for a bulletin board, but I declined. I didn't have the money to begin redoing the entire school, but I did offer that he could use the encyclopedias any time he wished.

❧

My students were as different from Thornhill students as was the new classroom. Some had never interacted with a white person, and they were shy or even scared. Language continued to be an obstacle, even though they were expected to have all classes in English from standard four on. As hard as I tried to say things the simplest way possible, a number of students never progressed. Most of them had no books or radios at home. When I brought *National Geographic* magazines to school, I watched a group of boys turn a picture one way and another trying to figure out what they were seeing. Looking at pictures is a learned skill—I had never realized that. Their knowledge of the outside world was minimal. Many had never traveled even as far away as Gaborone. One Saturday, Wayne and I took a group of students to the Gaborone Dam (no parental permission was required to ride on the open back of a pickup truck), and one boy asked in awe, "Is this the ocean?"

Discouragement set in. The lower achieving students caused disruptions because they didn't understand what was going on in class, and once they realized that I wouldn't be striking them on the hands with a ruler for misbehavior, they became even more rowdy. I had no idea how to curb them. I divided the class into ability groups for reading and maths, but it was hard, especially with so few resources, to keep the others occupied when I worked with one group. Each day felt like more of a challenge than I could face. I wanted to give up. We even talked about ending our term early and going back to the States, but instead I dragged myself on, day after day.

Miss Mogana, who taught standard one, often walked partway home with me—the African custom of seeing a visitor halfway home. Her keen eyes saw that I was lonely and unhappy, but she didn't bring that up. Instead, she simply walked with me and talked about the day's experiences or answered questions about village life. Occasionally, she stopped in for tea late in the afternoon after choir practice or sat with me in the Saturday evening English service in the big Lutheran church.

Then Aunt Esther came for a visit. She took a 6,000-mile detour on her way home from a year in Ethiopia. Her love of teaching, which was as great as my ambivalence, came to my rescue once again—not for learning multiplication tables in her curriculum library, but for help in teaching. She walked to school with me every day for three weeks, and while I taught one class, she taught another. She could never learn to pronounce some of the students' names, but they loved her anyway. With her assistance, I began to see new possibilities for making it through the year, and by the time she left, school felt more manageable. I even had enjoyable moments, but I was still happiest on non-school days.

The German pastor and his wife held a party to which some of the school teachers were invited. The headmaster arrived tipsy and proceeded to drink some more. He then began to complain loudly about the fact that I had fixed up my room but refused to do the same for others. Several embarrassed teachers ushered him out of the party, but I knew what he said was true. I had fallen back on my privilege in a way that disadvantaged others, with no thought to the way my actions would be perceived by them. I was dismayed when the host commented later that this outburst was the reason cross-cultural events didn't work. I knew that the mistake had been mine.

I came to the end of the school year (December), relieved and pregnant. I decided not to teach in the new term. Our baby would come in May, and then at the end of July we'd be packing to leave.

The morning my labor began, I walked to the hospital and then walked home again to get several things I wanted—a two-minute walk each way. Geoffrey was born early in the afternoon, and Wayne rushed off to send home telegrams to the waiting grandparents. Compared to hospitals in the States, everything here was casual. One neighbor who had been away for the morning returned and heard that I had gone to the hospital. She rushed over and stuck her head in the doorway of the labor and delivery room to ask how things were going. Without a word, the smiling midwife turned Geoffrey, whom she was still holding upside down by his feet, so our neighbor could see that he was a boy.

The next day, a group of girls from my former class came to the window of my hospital room to see the new baby. I brought him to the open, screenless, ground-level window, and they marveled at this little white baby, who was as much a novelty for them as their white, American teacher had been. Miss Mogana visited once we were home, and after she left, I discovered a baby rattle lying beside Geoffrey in his basket with a note that said, "From your Botswana Granny."

Mr. and Mrs. Semuli and Agatha wanted to have a farewell party for us at our house, proposing an evening two days before our departure. I didn't know what to say. By then most of our household would be packed up. I knew their homes were too small. Liesel, a single doctor at the hospital, solved the awkward situation by volunteering her house. Everyone gratefully agreed.

The day of the party, I looked out the window to see our three friends walking toward Liesel's house, one with a wooden case of soft drinks on her head. That was the first of several trips they made. I felt ashamed of my original lack of openness to their offer.

The party turned out to be marvelous, with lots of laughter, plentiful food, and loud music—a true Botswana gathering. Someone had been assigned to monitor the principal so he wouldn't go off script again. Everyone savored this last time together. It was late when Wayne and I walked home, leaving Liesel's house cluttered with party remains. Early the next morning, before I had even begun to think about going to clean up, I looked out to see our three friends, this time heading to Liesel's house with mop and broom in hand. I felt chagrined all over again that I had thought they didn't understand what they were asking of me as a host. Their generosity brought tears to my eyes.

I cried again two days later as we drove out of Ramotswa for the last time, wanting to hold forever in my mind each rondoval we passed, every scraggly thorn tree, and all the red rocks strewn across the landscape. I was leaving behind dear friends and bidding farewell to a unique part of my life. I was leaving our son's birthplace. Like everywhere else I had lived, it had become home and I loved it.

We turned onto the main road to Gaborone, which was only a little less bumpy than the one from the village. As I stared out at the barren landscape, I marveled at how I had changed in the past three years. I now saw subtle beauty in the surroundings that I once thought bare and uninteresting. I had been to places I hadn't known existed. I had done things that would have made me uncomfortable earlier.

There was the weekend soon after we arrived when I went with Wayne to a workshop he helped to lead. In the evening, women began a line dance, and one of them stepped out and pulled me in. "What do you mean, you can't dance?" she responded to my objection. "Everyone can dance." I smiled at how awkward I had been and at how good it felt to be accepted by those welcoming women.

I thought of one of the days Agatha and I walked home from school together. She had asked, "Do you think I should have a baby?" This question from a single woman startled me. Its answer had always been so assumed that it was never asked at home. Here things were different, and the certainties of Park View didn't necessarily apply. Here, few women remained unmarried and even fewer childless. A child offered the assurance of someone to care for one in old age. People didn't have retirement plans, and nursing homes did not exist. To be childless was risky. Miss Mogana, perhaps my best friend in Ramotswa, wasn't married and had two daughters. She was a leader at school and church, highly respected in the community. "You should do what you think is best," I had replied, my certainty gone. Now as I bumped along with Geoffrey in my lap, I mused about the way new realities cause us to ask new questions and consider different answers.

I joggled fussy Geoffrey and continued to think about going home—not just to Park View, but to the United States. It too was more of a home than I had recognized when I left it. Being with people from other countries had made me see that I wasn't as much on the fringes as I had always felt. I was thoroughly American. I had felt that when I went to the US Consulate for a Fourth of July potluck picnic and lined up my big green Tupperware bowl with all the other identical green Tupperware bowls. Once a British volunteer asked what sloppy joes were, and I had laughed with all the other Americans as we talked over each other explaining.

There was the afternoon I told the headmaster at Thornhill that I wasn't comfortable with a decision he had made. He had taken it as insubordination and, his lips trembling with anger, had said, "You know I can dismiss you." I had assumed that principals and teachers discussed options. I had been equally surprised when a highly trained European volunteer refused to change a light bulb. "I didn't come here to change light bulbs," he bristled. I, along with any American I knew, would have said, "Sure. Where's the ladder?"

Finally, Kgale Hill came into view, the landmark signifying that Gaborone was just ahead. Then we hit paved road and the ride smoothed out. I thought about the blue mountains of home and how much lay beyond them. I had tasted that beyond and wanted more.

26

Kentucky Again

I LOOKED OUT AT the hilly, green pasture where two young horses frisked around on a misty April afternoon. Wayne and I were visiting Harlan, Kentucky, where Wayne had been offered a job. He was about to finish the two-year graduate program in health care administration that he'd begun on our return from Botswana.

I had been happy in Easton, Maryland, where we had spent the previous year and wasn't at all sure I wanted to move again, particularly to a place that felt isolated. I was still reveling in being close to family, listening to classical radio stations, going to concerts, and finding the things I wanted in close-by stores. Harlan had none of these to offer. Instead, there was litter everywhere—along roads, up hillsides, and down creek banks. Shabby houses lined hollows or perched precariously on spindly stilts along steep banks and hillsides. Dreary house trailers stood in barren plots. There was one fast-food restaurant and one modest supermarket. The hospital building where Wayne's job would be seemed only a step up from prefabricated.

But poverty and lack, as obvious as they were, could not erase the beauty of this place. The energy of the horses was contagious, and the trees pushing their first gold and pink buds held the promise of a lush summer green that would drape hills and mountains. I had always been fascinated with the rich cultural heritage of the region and wanted to learn more about it. A small, mostly Mennonite group offered us a warm welcome and ongoing support. We could live a simpler, slower way of life than in some anonymous city, and this community's needs offered us many ways to contribute. We decided to accept the offer.

Wayne was attracted to the job, but for me there was another pull. As we had driven the roads that paralleled creek beds winding through narrow valleys, something deep within me softened and relaxed, something I hadn't even known was tight. This rugged eastern Kentucky geography drew me in and cradled me as no other place on Earth ever could. I was home.

In July, with the help of Wayne's family, we packed our belongings into a U-Haul truck and drove to Kentucky. We settled for the summer in a trailer park in the lowland next to Catron Creek, a hollow about as wide as the one where Lost Creek flowed and where I spent my earliest days. I was back in the heart of Appalachia. We lived next to a *crick*, and some of our friends lived up a *holler*. Almost every night, Loretta Lynn's voice carried through the humid air from our next-door neighbor's record player—"You Ain't Woman Enough (To Take my Man)." Her son Punky ("Punnn-ky") played with Geoffrey in the sandbox Wayne had built. Another neighbor's hunting hounds bayed, off and on, all day, and I watched, astonished, as other neighbors backed their pickup to the bank of Catron Creek, opened the tailgate, and shoved a load of trash down the bank toward the stream.

While life in this trailer park was novel to me, our small Mennonite group felt like home. All of us had grown up in Mennonite communities and had attended Mennonite colleges. Now most of us were health care providers working at the hospital. We gathered once a week, usually sharing a meal together before our meeting. We assisted each other in practical ways. When Wayne and I moved into our new house that fall, everyone turned out to carry boxes and later returned to help grade and seed our lawn. We helped paint another family's house. We gathered to process and freeze gunnysacks of corn and buckets of beans from our friend Bill's community-sized garden. Wayne and I traded childcare with the Millers, who lived across the railroad tracks from us.

I found great joy in mothering. I washed dishes and diapers, played with Fisher Price toys, read stories, listened to *Sesame Street* and *Mr. Rogers' Neighborhood*, canned tomatoes, froze peas, and made applesauce from the apple tree in our backyard. Being at home satisfied me on one level, but I often felt restless and was easily irritated. I was living my dream, so why was I easily out of sorts? Surely, it must be my failing—my impatience and selfishness.

Along with practical activities, our group engaged in heady, intense conversations about church and theology. Our goal was to be accountable to each other as we offered support emotionally, spiritually, and practically. Our discussions invigorated me, but Wayne felt less need for such interactions. I wanted him to be more active, but knew that he never had a lot to say, particularly in groups.

Wayne's lack of participation in our group was not all that concerned me. I couldn't understand his behavior. He was unhappy most of the time, absorbed with his job and some of the less than healthy dynamics there. When he came home, he was preoccupied and had little attention or energy for us. I alternated between trying to help him figure out how to cope at work and criticizing him for his lack of involvement in parenting and household chores. Then I would feel guilty for criticizing him and try to be understanding once again. We both struggled, together and separately. In spite of the medical and mental health expertise in our group, no one mentioned depression.

Fairly early in our time in Harlan, JoAnne offered to pray for our group five minutes each day. Several weeks later she reported in a meeting that she had received a message for two of us. She offered to speak with those two privately, to speak to the entire group, or to say nothing at all. We were all vaguely uncomfortable. This was an unusual experience for us, but we agreed that she should speak to the group since these insights had come through prayer for the group.

I was one of the two persons she named. I had no idea what she would say or whether it would ring true, but strangely I didn't feel anxious. She began by saying that the message for me made no sense to her because it seemed to be the opposite of what she observed. The message was that I was too dependent on Wayne and that I needed to depend less on him and to be more myself. How could she know that, I wondered? I understood her puzzlement because outwardly I was more outspoken than he, but inwardly, I constantly put out feelers for his mood. I carried his negativity, much as I had taken on Mother's worry. I had lost myself in an anxious muddle he and I created together.

That night as I lay in bed, I checked for the shame I thought I should feel at having my inner self revealed in such a public way, but I could find none. What had been said came from beyond the one who had prayed. I knew JoAnne hadn't made it up. She had been far too uneasy about speaking, as if she weren't sure she could trust what she had been given. But it was true. I felt not scolded or criticized but loved and surrounded by grace, seen personally by a Goodness too mysterious to be comprehended. I had been offered an insight I hadn't even known to ask for.

❦

After a year of trying, I became pregnant again. I battled nausea as I led a Sunday evening class at the Presbyterian church we attended, and I felt queasy as we cleaned what we called "flood mud" from the household belongings of Dick and Elaine, members of our group. An epic flood had washed through the region, coming within yards of our house but into the home of this family. We had never seen anything as persistently invasive as that mud. It seemed to find cracks and grooves we didn't even know existed. It was a relief to go home to a clean house that didn't reek of the bad-smelling mud.

Only weeks later I began spotting and was put on partial bed rest. I could manage most daily chores, but Melanie, a teenager in our group, came to clean for us, and Joan canned our tomatoes. Wayne did the grocery shopping. Geoffrey, who was already good at entertaining himself, drew pictures on big sheets of newsprint while I took long afternoon rests. From my bed I could hear the sporadic, almost musical plunks of felt-tip pens being dropped back into their tin can holder as he changed from one pen to another. It played an accompaniment to my sadness and guilt at not being able to be with him as much as usual.

One September evening, five weeks before the baby was due, we went to our usual weekly small-group meeting. Not long after we returned home, labor began and we rushed to the hospital because the doctors feared I might start bleeding again. On the way, we dropped off Geoffrey at the Millers'. The baby was born a little after three o'clock in the morning, and Wayne, eager to tell someone, rushed off to find Sara, a member of our group who was a nurse on night duty. Her mouth dropped open in surprise when he asked if she wanted to come and see our new baby. Only a few hours earlier we had been sitting together at our meeting, with no sign that the birth was imminent. Other than spending the first twenty-four hours in an incubator with oxygen for his rapid breathing, the baby was fine.

However, we were not prepared: the new baby had no name waiting for him. We had narrowed the list down to two possible boy names and three for a girl. The next day I sat cradling him in my arms and asked, "Are you a Matthew or a Jeremy?" He looked back at me but gave no sign of preference, so in the end we decided on Jeremy. What I hadn't known until we called my mother was that the day of his birth was my father's birthday. I was happy that this son, born in Kentucky as I had been, could share a commonality with the grandfather he would never meet.

❦

Sycamore trees grew along the river bottom and stood with white mottled trunks on the other side of the creek, our garden and lawn between. Every morning, standing at the sink with my hands in soapy dishwater and Jeremy clinging to my leg, I looked out at those trees. Sometimes they stretched up, open-armed, toward the sun. Other times fog caught in their branches like spider webs. On rare occasions, I saw a dramatic flash of red as a pileated woodpecker looked for bugs hidden under the bark. Most days there were only robins, bluebirds, cardinals, and all the little brown birds I lumped into one category.

The trees were still there in the evening, fading into the dark of the mountain behind them like sturdy ghosts, vigilant and unmoving. I counted on them, no matter what was going on in my life. Their solid trunks grounded me, and their constancy reassured me. Many days as I looked at them, I felt a restless longing that had nothing to do with them and everything to do with my own ill-defined searching. I would have been hard-pressed to say what it was that I wanted. All I knew was that I felt closed down, tight, inhibited by fears and insecurities. I wished for the magic prayer or insight or action that would free me instantly. I'd even have gone for a charismatic experience if that would have done the trick, but nothing ecstatic happened.

Through all of this, the sycamore trees stood steadfastly, and I began to notice how their branches opened out and reached up to the sky. It almost took my breath away. I stood in the kitchen and reached up my arms, but I couldn't breathe deeply enough to sustain that kind of a stretch. The trees were opening themselves to the light, to God, I told myself, and I couldn't. My insides felt like the cord-bound root ball of a nursery plant that has stood too long waiting to be planted, and I had no idea how to cut the cords.

The sycamores became my prayer. Their patient, wordless presence reminded me every day of what it was that I most longed for—to be open, unbound, fully alive. I didn't think about how many seasons of hot and cold, sun and wind those trees had grown through to become what I saw. I was impatient for growth to happen miraculously, instantaneously. I wanted change today, if not sooner. What was more, I didn't know how to make change happen. I knew I had a long way to go, and, not knowing what to do, I had to settle for what I had. Day by day those sycamore trees patiently prayed their prayer through me, and day by day I got out of bed, made breakfast, played with the boys, read another book, washed diapers, wrote in my journal, talked with friends, and looked out at those trees opening their arms to the sky.

⚘

I stretched out in our recliner as the afternoon sun filled the room with light. I breathed in the quiet and closed my eyes. Jeremy was asleep. Geoffrey was "resting" on his bed with a pile of books. I picked up my own book and paused to ponder before beginning to read. These afternoon interludes felt important to me. They weren't just quiet moments to myself but somehow preparation for an unknown future, so unknown I couldn't imagine it. I didn't want to say that to anyone because it felt presumptuous. What if that future never came? Yet I felt a certainty that something was growing in the dark, not yet ready to be exposed.

My reading centered on books about spirituality, prayer, silence, and meditation. Using these as tools for deepening one's faith had never been discussed in my growing up. My practical forebearers had spoken little of an interior life, seeing actions as the primary way faith should be expressed. I agreed that faith needs to be expressed outwardly, but I read hungrily about others' journeys into more awareness of God's presence—books by Elizabeth O'Connor, Morton Kelsey, Thomas Merton, and Henri Nouwen.

While I could not yet see where I was heading, I was not without clues. In my journal I commented about becoming more conscious of interest in people. On one occasion I wrote, "In thinking of my talents/gifts one that stands out . . . is my love and interest in people—I'm not sure exactly what all that means except I recognize that many of my feelings of being stifled, my restless feelings . . . are due to a lack of using that gift."

Another time I wrote, "I often experience an intense yet vague feeling of wanting to touch [others'] hurts and disappointments . . . I really admire and almost envy this quality [of caring] when I see it in others."

During the summer after the flood, our group made the decision to form a congregation and have church services of our own on Sunday mornings, a move we had been considering for some time. As a part of this new house church, I had plenty of opportunities for involvement. I helped plan the themes for our worship services and occasionally gave the sermon, although I didn't think of it as such: I was just speaking on a topic or scripture text. I participated in planning and leading church retreats. I taught a Sunday school class. There were few parts of our church life in which I was not involved. Yet I would have been surprised had someone told me I was participating in leadership roles. I was just doing things that interested me.

Wayne had become restless in his job and determined to begin looking for a new one in the spring, but I was reluctant at the thought of leaving Harlan. On Christmas Day 1979, he received an unexpected call asking him to consider taking the administrator position at a Mennonite nursing home in Chambersburg, Pennsylvania. The following week, while we were visiting family in Harrisonburg, Wayne and I took a day to drive there for a visit. Wayne was excited about this new possibility, and I reluctantly agreed that it would be a good move for him. Moving was always hard for me, but I'd figure out how to make it work.

In the middle of packing, a call came from Harrisonburg saying that Grandpa had collapsed with a brain aneurism and was in the hospital. Two days later, on a Sunday morning before we were fully awake, Mother called to say he had died. I hung up the phone and sobbed in Wayne's arms. Grandpa, the anchor of my childhood world, was gone.

We had been losing him gradually as he sank into dementia, but I treasured one memory from the recent past. We were visiting in Virginia and two-year-old Jeremy woke from his nap, still feeling cuddly. I carried him into the study where Grandpa sat, doing nothing. He looked up at us and smiled, his blue eyes crinkling in the old familiar way that I hadn't seen for a long time. "Hello, Jeremy," he said. It was as if the old Grandpa were back, the vibrant person I had known most of my life. I held that rare moment of lucidity as a gift.

We drove to Harrisonburg for the funeral, and afterword, Wayne and I drove back to Harlan to finish packing and loading our U-Haul. The boys stayed with Mother. As we drove into the Kentucky hills, I grieved not only Grandpa's passing but the little house on Catron Creek that we were about to leave. It had been home for the past three years, and I'd assumed we would live there much longer. Maybe if I wouldn't allow myself to settle in so completely, I wouldn't find moving so difficult, I thought to myself. But I loved this place—the white-blooming "sarvus" (serviceberry) trees and redbud of early spring, the lush summer nights alive with crickets and fireflies, bluebirds in our apple trees, the protective hills, the mist-cloaked valleys, and the white-trunked sycamores. I knew I would carry this beauty within me. It would be a part of me forever.

27

Chambersburg

As we drove north on Route 11, the Shenandoah Valley opened like a reverse funnel, spilling us out of narrow confines into the broad Cumberland Valley, where the blue mountains retreated to finger-thin lines on the horizon. From the highway red barns, blue silos, and old farmhouses were visible, separated by wide fields of grain. Thrifty Pennsylvania farmers had little tolerance for untidy fence lines where wild flowers could grow or birds pause to sing. Every inch was planted. We passed through small towns occasionally, and then farms took over the landscape again. Little caught my interest, even though I was driving to my new home. Surely there had to be more here than I noted from the road, more to be discovered. At least I hoped so.

But from my new kitchen window I saw much the same: not white sycamores against an overgrown hillside but a flat, well-manicured field, newly sprayed for killing dandelions. Our yard was weedless. Off to the side I could see the trim main entrance to the nursing home—brick with an overhanging entrance and white cupola—where Wayne was working. A tidy collection of resident cottages spread beyond it. On the other side of the road lay a large dairy farm. Everywhere neatness prevailed, except for the Conococheague (*kah*-no-*kah*-cheeg), a stream bordering the nursing home. It was the nearest wild spot, with lush grasses growing at its edge. I said its name over and over because I liked the rhythmic, musical sound—*Conococheague, Conococheague, Conococheague.*

Left to right: **Geoffrey, Jeremy, Wayne, and me in Chambersburg.**

After being outsiders in a poor area of Appalachia, we were now part of a prosperous Mennonite community where I once again met people who knew my family. Our house, which came with the job, was like the people who built it: rather plain in appearance but evidencing wealth—solid cherry kitchen cabinets, thick carpets, a built-in china cupboard, large windows, generous bathrooms, and lots of closets. The only thing it lacked was an aesthetically pleasing layout. The fireplace was positioned so close to a corner of the family room that we couldn't group chairs around it; the windowless dining room nook felt dreary; and the black asphalt patio extended to the walls of the house in a suffocating way, leaving no softening margin for flower beds or shrubbery. An equally black driveway dominated the entrance to the house.

How could I complain, though, with such a well-built house? Nursing home maintenance men came to fix any problem, from refrigerator malfunctions to a rat making midnight raids in our kitchen. The lawn was mowed for us and snow shoveled. I rode on a bus with residents to the grocery store. It felt like a promised land.

I missed much about Kentucky, but Chambersburg seemed to be a land of milk and honey—abundance everywhere. The dairy farm across the fields operated a state-of-the-art milking parlor that the boys and I sometimes visited. Corn towered over our heads in midsummer, and fields of wheat progressed from yellow-green to gold. On my weekly trip to the farmers' market, Jeremy helped me decide which cheeses to buy and waited impatiently while I chose bunches of locally grown beets, fat cabbage heads, and fresh, leafy lettuce. Nearby orchards offered apples and peaches, which I bought by the bushel. At another orchard a few miles away, we picked cherries ourselves, climbing tall ladders into branches hanging so heavy with fruit I could hardly stop picking.

The retirement community welcomed us warmly, delighted to have young children around. Our sons gained dozens of doting "grandparents," and Wayne and I were treated like favorite children. We were taken out for meals by residents, given small gifts, and warmly welcomed to social events. Our house being on the entrance drive gave us high visibility. When a resident told me that she and others sat in the sunroom watching Geoffrey and Jeremy play in our backyard, I wasn't sure how to feel. I understood their enjoyment at watching children play, but I also felt exposed. There was no place outside where we weren't on display.

I knew we couldn't find a church that offered the compatibility we felt with our small Harlan group, but after weeks of visiting Mennonite churches in the area, we settled on the least conservative one. We liked Tom and Elaine, the young pastor and his wife, who welcomed us and seemed eager to become friends, but I noted that even in this church the significant leadership positions were all held by men.

In Harlan, I had read Elizabeth O'Connor's book about the Church of the Savior in Washington, D.C., a group who "do church" in nontraditional ways. One story that stood out vividly was their long and challenging process of creating Dayspring, a silent retreat center near Damascus, Maryland. The idea of a silent retreat appealed to me—having time for reading, meditation, and prayer without distractions or chatter. Their efforts to incorporate art into the center made it even more compelling. This was a place I wanted to go, and Maryland was now next door.

Settling in took time, but after a year of adjustment, I was ready to try something new. I wrote a letter to Dayspring requesting information. Even that step felt like a venture into the unknown. When the materials arrived, I looked over the schedule of retreats the way a hungry diner peruses a menu. Everything looked good. I wanted to attend all the retreats, but I finally settled on a journaling one. Even so, I found my heart beating fast as I filled out the registration form and handed it to Wayne to mail.

I watched him walk up the hill to his office where we posted our mail. What have I done now, I wondered?

The weekend finally came. I drove through the early summer countryside feeling that I was on an adventure into a world completely unlike anything I had ever experienced. I was about to meet people who had sophisticated jobs in Washington, people whose lives were surely much different from mine. True, I had met some such people in Gaborone, Botswana, which was so small that all Americans, including consulate staff, rubbed shoulders sooner or later. That had been happenstance. Now I was inserting myself into a world I never thought I'd enter.

Dayspring was as lovely as I'd expected. Most of one wall in the large meeting room was taken up with a stone fireplace and hearth. Large windows looked out at woods and open meadow. Books lined built-in shelves, cushioned chairs offered comfortable seating, and pieces of original artwork hung on the walls. Light poured into the dining room through large windows, highlighting the grain of the wooden tables. One could simply sit here and feast on the natural light, I thought. My individual bedroom was simple, small, and comfortably furnished, but having a room all to myself made it feel luxurious beyond words.

As we gathered for the opening session of the retreat, no one gave a hint that I didn't fit in. I felt more comfortable than I had expected. Before we entered the silence, we were asked to come up with an image representing where we saw ourselves at that point in our lives. I immediately pictured a fledgling on the edge of a nest, wanting to fly and being afraid. I could picture the small bird, timidly flapping its wings, pausing, flapping them again but not with enough force to take off. This image sounded clichéd, but it was what had come to me.

I knew I was facing challenges in my life, especially at church, where a woman leading a small group or teaching an adult Sunday school class was seen as questionable: women were not to teach men. I felt hemmed in by this. I wasn't so much afraid of the idea of nudging those boundaries as I was lacking in confidence. Wayne had inherited from his parents' Amish background a reluctance to do anything that would make him stand out. He magnified my doubts with his fear that I might appear foolish or awkward or fail completely. He wanted me to play a quiet role that would offer no opportunity for me to look foolish or fail.

When I met for a private session with the retreat leader, he encouraged me to take more risks, saying that when people use their gifts, it usually frees others to use theirs as well. My pushing ahead might free Wayne too. Never before had anyone encouraged me to take risks.

On the last afternoon, I lay out in the warm grass and watched an inchworm slowly make its way up one grass blade—drawing its feet up behind its front ones and then waving its front end in the air looking for a next step. It was easy for me to see where it should land its feet; not so the worm. I too felt like I was waving in the air, not sure where to land. I wondered if there was a perspective from which my next step appeared simple and obvious. I wished I could see it or that someone would point it out to me.

Our small group from church was not going well. Joe, who had been leading it, was floundering, and I had been toying with the idea of offering to lead. I was not sure how well I could do it, but after the retreat I decided I should try. Wayne objected. Joe was a good friend, he pointed out, and I might offend him by my offer. I should let things run their course. I didn't need to intervene. Joe had talked to us about feeling discouraged, so I didn't think he would be offended. I suspected that the real reason for Wayne's opposition was his fear of my failure.

One evening Tom and Elaine visited us, and I broached the topic. "I have something I want to talk about," I said, "the leadership of our small group." I held my breath, not being sure how Wayne would react. To my relief, he said nothing. "I am really frustrated, and I'd like to offer to lead the group, but Wayne doesn't want me to." Again, Wayne said nothing, so I continued.

"I don't know what to do . . . It's really hard to hold back . . . I can hardly sit there and watch Joe flounder." To my surprise, I started to cry. I hadn't realized how deeply I felt about this. "It's not that I'm sure I can do it," I continued after a pause. "I'm scared to try and yet, somehow, I feel like I need to."

"I don't like the idea of her offering to lead," Wayne said. "I'm afraid it would offend Joe, and I don't want that to happen . . . Besides, I'm not sure I want to be in a group she is leading. If she does, I think I'd probably stop attending."

Tom and Elaine listened and asked questions. Then Tom said, "Kathie, if you have the urge to try it, I think you should." Then he turned to Wayne and said, "And I think it would be a mistake for you, Wayne, to

withdraw your support from Kathie by not attending." Wayne said nothing. Afterward I told Wayne that I would offer to lead the group. Again,
he was silent.

That night I had a dream. Wayne and I were looking at the dug-out
basement of a house under construction. It was surrounded by mud and
all sorts of discarded wood scraps and other debris. I wanted to leave, so
I started toward the doorway, where a plank was laid across the debris to
solid ground.

"Oh, no, you can't go out there," Wayne said to me. "It's not safe."

"It's OK. I can make it," I replied.

"Kathie, you can't. You'll get hurt," he said even more emphatically,
but I continued toward the doorway. Just when I got there a workman appeared. He held out his hand to me and I took it and easily walked across
the board to solid ground.

The next day when I called Joe to let him know I would be willing
to lead the group, he sounded relieved. When I told Wayne, he again said
nothing but was grumpy the rest of the evening.

At our next meeting, I offered to take over leadership and Joe gave
me his blessing. As a result, one couple left the group because they believed it was wrong for a woman to teach men. Everyone else remained.
Our group functioned well, and Wayne and I continued our friendship
with Joe and his wife—if anything, closer than before. Wayne and I didn't
talk about my leadership. I knew he needed some time to get used to
me in this new role, and I needed time to build my confidence. If more
discussion was needed, it could come later.

28

What Will I Do Next?

I STRETCHED LUXURIOUSLY, HOVERING between sleep and waking, allowing my mind to trickle into the day. I needed to get up, make breakfast, and send Geoffrey off to school. *School.* "I surely am glad I don't need to face a classroom full of noisy children today," I said to myself. I'd said this before, but now it woke me up. "Kathie," I thought out loud, "if you still feel relief *six years* after teaching, that should tell you something—you *really* don't want to teach."

Why had that not occurred to me before? It seemed so obvious. But I knew the answer, even as I asked the question. I had no idea what I *did* want to do. Teaching had been my default option after eliminating other careers. I had wanted to stay at home. Mother told me I was more domestic than academic, and I didn't question that. She was right that I enjoyed domestic activities more than my sisters and academic pursuits less than they did. But the reality looked different now that I faced a coming time when the boys would be grown and I'd have little to do. I knew that I would become bored.

I began to pay attention to things I might enjoy, but I eliminated each because it required going back to school and I did not want to go to school again. The question of what to do next continued to float around in the back of my mind as I walked my exercise route around the retirement home or vacuumed the living room floor.

I sometimes accompanied Wayne to business conferences, and I began to glean new ideas from them. At a conference in Louisville, Kentucky, a shopping trip was offered for wives of attendees, but the chaplaincy division of the conference included a workshop led by Wayne

Oates. He would be talking about pastoral care. I'd never heard of him, but the topic sounded interesting. As I sat and listened to the presentation, I felt energized. I could get excited about the kind of work he spoke of, but that would require schooling. Besides, it appeared to be a man's world, if his audience was any indication.

At another conference, I attended a workshop on creating a children's day-care program on the same campus as a retirement home. The idea was to develop intergenerational activities to benefit both children and elders. I could see many advantages in this arrangement, so I mentioned it to Kay, the nursing home social worker. Just before my Dayspring retreat, she and I drove several hours to visit a retirement home day-care program. Along the way, we discussed my questions about future work.

Once there, we observed classes and talked with teachers, children, and senior residents. Then we met the administrator, who explained the program's structure. Just as she was describing the job of coordinating activities between children and residents, she was called out of the room for a moment. While we waited, I turned to Kay and said, "That will be my role, coordinating those activities."

Kay laughed. "I don't know why you say you don't know what you will do," she responded. "I think you were made for this!" I felt a surge of hope. A job like this wouldn't require more schooling. Maybe what I wanted was possible. Maybe I could find something I liked without more schooling. Wayne's nursing home board was not interested in establishing a day-care program, but Kay continued to encourage me to explore.

After another conference where I attended a session on setting up support groups for families of residents, I came home with a sheaf of papers to show Kay. She invited me to help structure and lead such a group. I found it easy to plan with her, but actually leading was another matter. Before the first session, I wrote out copious notes, afraid to leave any part unscripted. By the end of the evening, my mouth was completely dry and my cheeks brilliant red, but I had made it through without a major stumble. Each meeting became easier, and I began to look forward to those evenings. The added bonus was that Wayne had the boys in bed by the time I got home and I returned to a quiet, peaceful house.

29

New Life

WHEN JEREMY WAS ONLY months old, I began to realize that I wanted a third child. When I told Wayne he said, "Definitely not." It was at the height of his depression and he felt overwhelmed by our two. Over the next several years we talked about it from time to time. As his depression lifted, his "no" gradually moved to "maybe" and then to "yes." By then, we had been in Chambersburg for a year. When I became pregnant, we were both excited, but our happiness was short-lived. Days after we told Mother and my sisters, I lost the baby. At nine weeks, the doctor didn't see a reason for me to come in for an office visit. If it was that minor, I told myself, why should I make a big deal of it? I couldn't think of a good way to tell people about it when they hadn't even known I was pregnant, so I told only my closest friends and tried to go on as if nothing had happened.

Then came a different kind of loss. Tom and Elaine announced that they were leaving for three years to work in Tanzania. Not only would we be losing our best friends, we would also be without Tom's gifted pastoral leadership. I was excited for them but sad about their leaving.

The church began a pastoral search as Tom and Elaine made their preparations to leave, and I found it more interesting than I expected. One Sunday a large group of us sat in a Sunday school room and made a list on the blackboard of what we wanted in a new pastor. As I read the list, I mentally checked off the things I'd like to do and also noted the ones I might be capable of. "I could do most of those," I mused to myself, but I immediately dismissed the thought as arrogant. I was glad no one could read my mind. Who do you think you are, anyway? I scolded myself. You have no training, and you have small boys at home. Besides, the church would not consider a woman. I pulled myself back into the discussion going on around me.

As sometimes happens in pastoral searches, a faction developed within the congregation: a group of older men felt strongly that we should follow the traditional practice of choosing someone from within the congregation. Not only that—they knew who that person should be. I didn't agree with them, nor did I like the way they seemed to push their wishes on others. I found myself thrown into a turmoil I couldn't understand. I was blindsided by how frantic, angry, and almost desperate I felt. I was grieving my miscarriage and the loss of Tom and Elaine. I knew that my hormones were not yet back to normal, but this seemed beyond that.

I was too emotionally involved. I couldn't talk myself down. Over and over, I rehearsed my arguing points. They all ended at the same place: I feared that this group saw their favorite candidate as someone they could control. He might have the gifts needed, but he wasn't prepared for the role. He was too young. He needed more time.

Then one Sunday evening at church as we stood for prayer, a member of this group stated to the congregation that he believed the next pastor was among us at that moment. I felt a flash of anger at this seeming manipulation, and almost simultaneously a jolt of energy ran through my body, as if I had touched a live wire. What if I were to speak up and say, "It's me"? My fingers tingled as I gripped the bench in front of me. Where in the world did that thought come from? I dismissed it even before the declaration was fully formed. I didn't want to think it, let alone say it to anyone, not even Wayne.

A week later, early on a December morning, I sat on the yellow couch in our living room, which was bright with light from the picture windows at either end of the room. No one else was up yet, and I settled into the quiet before my day began. I read the story of the angel coming to Joseph and telling him, "Do not fear to take Mary your wife, for that which is conceived in her is of the Holy Spirit" (Matt. 1:20b, RSV). As I read those words, I knew, with as much clarity as if an angel were standing in front of me, that these words were being spoken to me, scared and confused as I was. The turmoil in my "womb" was "conceived of the Holy Spirit." This was not my usual way of talking, but the meaning was what mattered. I did not need to be afraid of the swirling mass of emotions inside me. It had meaning because God was somehow present in it. I didn't need to understand, but neither did I need to be fearful. I had no idea what this meant, and I certainly didn't have the courage to talk about it with anyone, so, like Mary, I stored it away inside myself. My one comfort was the angel's words, "Do not fear." I relaxed a bit, feeling the warmth of the sun. Today, at least, all I needed to do was focus on the tasks at hand—preparations for Christmas.

Tom and Elaine came to stay with us the week before they left. I was glad for this time with them and also glad that we were the ones who got to drive them to the airport in New York. We borrowed a van to accommodate their luggage and drove through feeble January sunshine to get there.

On our way home, snow swirled around us, making the roads more and more slippery. Wayne and I were tense because of the poor driving conditions. The boys were tired. All of us felt sad and bereft. By the time we got home, Geoffrey had a fever and my throat hurt almost too much to swallow. It took us weeks to feel better.

I became pregnant, and again, just after beginning to tell family members our good news, I miscarried. This time I grieved as I had not allowed myself to the first time, now for both lost babies. These two tiny potentialities had been snuffed out and would never grow to maturity. Who were these little beings that we had lost? What would they have contributed to our family and to the world? We'd never know.

There would be no other baby, I determined. I would not let myself go through this again. Clearly there was a problem, although the doctor assured me that two miscarriages did not necessarily mean anything was wrong. Impulsively I sent many of the baby things I had been saving to a thrift store and then spent a sleepless night regretting having done so. I contemplated going to reclaim everything the next day, but I knew that wasn't an option. Like my babies, those things were gone.

I felt angry and empty. I had asked for clarity about having another child. Wayne had had a change of heart. It all seemed so right, so much an answer to my prayers, but it wasn't to be. What use was prayer? Why should I pray, now that the answer I thought was so clear had ended in emptiness? Once more I sat on our yellow couch with the light streaming into the room and felt numb. Then a thought came to my mind, clearly formed. I heard no words, but the message was clear: *You can ask for new life.*

New life? Hadn't I just been denied that, not once but twice? Was this just a clever wordplay that sounded pious but held little meaning? I had no idea, but the thought persisted. God would never turn away a request for new life, I reasoned. The new life of a baby wasn't going to happen. Maybe there were other kinds of new life. I didn't know what else to ask for—I wasn't even sure there was use in asking for anything—but I prayed for new life, not expecting much.

❧

Something new happened, but not anything that looked like new life to me. One Friday evening in May Wayne came home from work and suggested that we pour glasses of lemonade and sit on the patio. That was strange. He wasn't usually given to a leisurely pause before dinner, but the boys were busy playing and it seemed a nice idea. I sensed he had something important to tell me, so I waited expectantly. As soon as we were seated, he handed me an envelope. My stomach did a flip. Something about this felt ominous. I opened the envelope slowly, took out the letter and read the request for Wayne to resign from his job. I looked at him in wordless shock, in disbelief.

I knew things had not been going well at work. The nursing home's founder had retired from his business and created an office for himself across the hallway from Wayne's office. Privately, we joked that his huge, ornate desk looked like a casket, but the problems were no laughing matter. Wayne had been trying to extricate himself from a power struggle with the founder and a prominent board member, both of whom wanted to micromanage Wayne's work. I hadn't thought it was this serious, but I was wrong.

What would this mean? We had planned to raise our sons here. We had assumed this job would last for many years to come. I had worked hard over the past three years to make a place for myself in the community, and finally I was feeling at home. My roots had taken hold, and the last thing in the world I wanted was to move.

We somehow got through supper, through the restless night, through the weekend. As the news spread, many people expressed support, but the fact remained—we had to move. We slowly stumbled out of the fog. Wayne began to put out feelers for a new job. The retirement home assured us that we could stay in our house until we found a new place or job, but we didn't want to hang around.

We had lost our best friends, our hoped-for babies, and now Wayne's job and the house that went with it. I had just dug new flower beds and we had planted strawberries. What was this all about? If this was new life, I didn't like it. I spent time sitting on the bank of the Conococheague reading, thinking, crying.

Don and Lorraine, friends from church, invited us to their house one evening for a picnic supper. After the meal, we adults sat in lawn chairs in the fading light while the children ran around playing tag. Our conversation turned to Wayne's and my future. Wayne had a lead or two, but we had no clear sense of where we wanted to go. My only clarity was that I wanted to stay where we were. I looked around at Lorraine's tidy lawn bordered by flower beds and the house that had been in their family for years. Lorraine commented that she couldn't imagine moving anywhere else, and I felt a wave of envy. Both of their families lived nearby, and their friends were mostly long-term ones. I wanted a safe, familiar world like theirs. I wanted to be settled. We had moved often enough— seven times in the past twelve years. It was our turn to be settled. How was it that we had to leave when they could stay?

Back at our house the next day, I looked out the window and pictured myself digging with my bare hands deep into the freshly turned soil of the new flower bed. I imagined dirt under my nails and fists full of the red-brown clay, holding on with all my strength. What accompanied that image was another that I didn't want to acknowledge. The image itself came from a children's book: a picture of a giant picking up a small boy in his hand and holding him high. The boy, not realizing that the giant was friendly, was flailing his arms and legs. I saw a similar hand gently picking me up as I kicked and screamed in protest. I didn't want to believe that hand could be loving or that it could place me somewhere better than this. Even so, I was not able to shake the feeling that there was love and grace hidden somewhere in all of our confusion.

In spite of myself, I began to have moments of excitement about moving to a new place. I knew the petty issues surrounding Wayne's job would soon be insignificant to us, and a new setting held the possibility of freedom Wayne hadn't felt in a while. A new house to decorate always excited me, as did the possibility of new friends. I threw myself into the work of transition, trusting that as bereft as I felt while preparing to move, life would not always feel this bleak.

30

Back to Virginia

WE DROVE BETWEEN GREEN pastures with the car windows wide open. The fence rows, ragged with tall grasses, provided observation perches and swinging rides for red-winged black birds and meadowlarks. The fragrance of sun-warmed soil and freshly mowed grass filled my lungs, and when we passed honeysuckle I breathed in even more deeply. Crickets and cicadas chirped. Virginia in summertime—could there be anything better? I held my hand out the window, letting it swoop and soar in the air from the fast-moving car. I was coming home, not to Rockingham County, where I grew up with mountains surrounding me, but back to Virginia. Part of me exulted in the sunny day. Another part of me was grieving this move that neither Wayne nor I had chosen. I hadn't imagined ever living here again, but Virginia pulled me in with its irresistible summer charms.

The countryside shifted from rural to more residential. We drove through the edge of the Manassas battlefield where more than a hundred years ago soldiers in blue and gray had faced off two times. The now-peaceful green fields were bounded by split-rail fences and punctuated by markers commemorating soldiers or maneuvers. Then, rather abruptly, we were on Sudley Road, the main commercial thoroughfare of the city of Manassas. We passed car dealerships, motels, restaurants, strip malls, and more fast-food places than existed in all of Chambersburg—a plethora of shopping opportunities after the stand-alone Sears and J.C. Penney stores we were leaving behind.

In this town everything was new to me. I belonged to no recognizable community as I had in Chambersburg. There was no Mennonite church, no one I knew. The nursing home Wayne would now administer was several miles away from our home rather than a hundred yards up the hill, so he wouldn't be coming home for lunch, and I wouldn't be learning to know staff and residents. I would need to develop a community apart from his work.

Yet I was in Virginia, and I loved our new house. It was a brick 1950s Cape Cod positioned on a generous corner lot with a green lawn and a large Norway maple like the ones around Grandpa's house. The inside reminded me of Mother's house, only nicer. There was a fireplace in the living room, an open stairway with a graceful bannister leading to the three bedrooms on the second floor, and hardwood floors, some of them carpeted. The dining room included a built-in corner cupboard, and the den, all knotty pine, had built-in bookshelves. True, the kitchen was inconveniently arranged, but that we could fix, and there was a partially finished basement, where we could put canning shelves and a washer and dryer. There was a wash line in the middle of the backyard.

Our first night there, I made one final trip downstairs to check that the doors were locked. On my way back upstairs to our sleeping bags on the floor, I paused on the stairway to survey the empty, expectant living room. I happened to see myself reflected in the mirror above the fireplace mantle. There I stood, my hand resting on the rail like a Southern belle in a gracious mansion. I could hardly believe that it was me.

The following day, when the moving truck arrived and we began positioning furniture and unpacking boxes, I saw only the reality of all the work needing to be done. Within a week or two I tackled the multipaned windows that looked like they hadn't been washed in years. As I leaned out our bedroom window, three floors above ground level at the side of the house, my new neighbor Rosa called up to me saying that it was good to see the house being loved again. When she stopped in to visit a few days later, she said that I had already made the house more of a home than it had ever been before, and she had seen it being built. I knew then that Rosa would be a good friend.

Jim and Pam, friends from Chambersburg, came a few days after we moved, their pickup loaded with plants, both indoor ones and starts from the relatively new outside beds at our last house. I had never been a great gardener. Every place we lived I had planted a few flowers, but the only things that ever flourished were weeds. Yet I kept trying, lured on by the pictures I carried in my head of English cottage gardens. I wanted to try again despite the unpromising red clay and the dry Virginia summers. Jim labored that hot day, taking off sod and digging into the hard soil to create our first flower bed.

Later in the fall I tackled the dead barberry bushes covered by honeysuckle vines that were growing behind a retaining wall. Removing honeysuckle from anything is challenging, but when the "anything" is stickery barberry, it is even harder. I finally managed to dig out the bushes and then worked on the honeysuckle roots. "It's impossible to get rid of honeysuckle," Rosa commented, shaking her head, when she came home from the grocery store and saw me digging. That made me more determined than ever. I couldn't allow my future flowers to suffer the same fate as the barberry bushes. So I dug on and on, down to the bottom of the four-foot-high wall. It took several days to complete, and I reported to Rosa that I had found a new definition for infinity—honeysuckle roots.

31

A Path Emerges

WE WERE NOW MEMBERS of Northern Virginia Mennonite Church in Fairfax, half an hour from Manassas. I began participating in small ways, trying to figure out where I might fit in. Over the next year, I became more involved than I ever had been in Chambersburg. I taught an adult Sunday school class, which didn't surprise me, but then I was asked to lead a small group, and then to be worship leader—the person who planned and led the liturgy each week.

Wayne and I had long, intense discussions about his discomfort with my new responsibilities. I wanted to push ahead, but my confidence was shaky. Loren, our pastor, and Jay and Shirley, our closest friends from church, supported me and kept nudging me toward trying more and more. Wil, the wise "elder" of the congregation, smiled and said quietly, "Gifts that are given are to be used." I wasn't sure what they saw, but I wanted to believe them. Shirley especially kept encouraging me to go back to school. I didn't want to.

During our second summer in Manassas, we spent a week at the beach with Shirley and Jay. Most mornings I got up early to walk alone on the beach as the clouds changed from gray to shades of pink, salmon, and gold before the sun itself slipped soundlessly over the horizon. I loved the fresh, smooth sand—as yet unmarred by the footprints or sandcastles that the day would bring—and the cool air lingering from the night. The sound of waves filled me with an odd juxtaposition of calm and energy, a dynamic background to my wandering thoughts. One morning I sat down on a grassy hummock to look out at the tireless ocean, which continued its slow but powerful motion, as it had for millennia.

My life seemed a grain of sand compared to the vast scene before
me. I thought of my puny fears and my deep longings, how they met like
the shore and the ever-forceful waves. I knew I could resist the inevitable
no longer. I said out loud, "OK, if I *have* to go back to school again, I
will." I could muster no enthusiasm. The waves continued, their muffled
roar washing over my fears. What this would mean, I had no idea, and
being on vacation, I didn't want to think about it further. But the words
had been said, and like the imperceptible moment when the tide shifts,
I knew that a subtle change had occurred. It took only a few weeks for it
to evidence itself.

One late-summer afternoon the phone rang. It was Loren. "Kathie,"
he said, "the seminary [Eastern Mennonite Seminary, part of Eastern
Mennonite College in Harrisonburg] is offering an extension course in
Northern Virginia, as they do every year, and they have said that each
congregation may send only two or three people for this class. You are
the first person who comes to my mind for taking the course. What do
you think?"

"Yes, I'll do it," I responded, not even pausing to consider and only
then thinking to ask, "What is it about?"

"It's for congregational leaders, to help them develop resources and
practices for spiritual growth," he replied. We discussed the particulars
of when and where. Loren said he planned to attend, so we could ride
together. That evening I wrote in my journal:

> I marvel in the change this year has brought. Last fall when the
> seminary course was announced, my first thought was that I
> would never have the nerve to drive to Maryland for an evening
> class. Secondly, I would never have the courage to take a semi-
> nary course. I envied the people who did but felt that it wasn't
> for me. Now I am actually excited by the prospect . . . It's all a
> little overwhelming.

The class offered me the opportunity to begin to explore some of my
inner urgings and interests. We were each required to keep a journal to
be turned in weekly. The next week we got the past week's writing back
along with comments by the teacher. For the first time, I had someone
responding to my inner process.

We each had an individual conference with the teacher as well. He began mine by saying, "What I note in your writing is that you have an unusually strong sense of call—an urgency to be moving forward. Does that sound accurate to you?" I must have looked puzzled because he went on to explain, "Given ten average people in a congregation, you would be more concerned than they are about spiritual growth and the life of the church."

"I guess so," I said. "I never thought of it like that."

"No, you might not have, but it stands out to me."

"I know there are times when I wish I could just be satisfied taking care of my family, but something in me keeps pushing ahead."

"What do you think that something is?"

"I don't know. I question that a lot." I paused. "Is it God calling me, or is it pride or competitiveness?"

"Those are important questions to ask, questions we all need to constantly keep before us," he said. We talked about that and then he asked, "Do you have a sense of what you are being called to do?"

"I don't, but I'm beginning to wonder if it is more that I am afraid to know. I find myself thinking more and more about seminary, but that scares me. I can't really see myself as a pastor."

Later, our conversation kept coming back to me. Why couldn't I just be satisfied with the status quo? Why did staying at home no longer feel like enough? I wished it would.

❧

I sat in a silence broken only by the soft rustle of someone changing position or an occasional crack or pop from a burning log in the large stone fireplace. I looked out the window to the drab, leafless trees. I was at Dayspring again, this time for a daylong Advent retreat.

The retreat leader offered us pastels to use, suggesting that drawing might be a helpful way to express our inner thoughts. I drew slowly, hesitantly, not sure what I wanted to do. A translucent flower bud appeared, just on the cusp of opening. Even though the bud was drawn as closed, the colors I used suggested what lay within—pink, green, and yellow. In my journal, I wrote, "Much of my life is like the color hidden deep within a blossom, there but unrealized by any but me . . . It's covered by the drab outer leaves that to me look rather dead. If I strip them away suddenly, the forming flower may die. I sometimes rebel at the slow growth, but life keeps calling me."

I became almost teary with longing. I sensed vibrant, swirling color within me, pulsing and flowing. All I could see on the outside was brown, not even green. I felt like a paper bag containing a bottle of spirits—vitality hidden in a plain brown wrapper. I couldn't dance that beauty into the world or paint what I visualized. Neither could I make music as expressive as what I felt. I didn't know what to do other than continue my daily life and trust that the opening would occur.

෯

Jeremy had started first grade and was now gone for the entire school day. Some days I wandered aimlessly around the house, not quite sure what to do with myself and not at all sure how to begin figuring out the rest of my life. I could no longer pretend that changes would not come. In addition, I still felt fragile from the series of losses the past two years had brought. I wrote in my journal:

> I feel pregnant, very pregnant. The life within me is moving, kicking, elbowing, but what is it? I am impatient for it to be born, to learn to know what it is that I am carrying. I try to identify each movement . . . but it is covered, an unidentifiable shape. Restlessly I try to encourage each movement, hoping it holds the key to bringing forth the new life I know is hidden within. I am alternately filled with anticipation of something about to happen and discouragement, wondering how long this false labor . . . has to last before the real labor begins.
> My life has so many questions and so few answers. Why can't I have more children? Why am I here? What should I do with my time and energy? . . . How can I be more faithful in my own little world of routine and responsibility?

I decided to work my way through the book *Transforming Bible Study* by Walter Wink. In the preface, Wink describes this method of Bible study as a melding of biblical studies and Jungian psychology, saying that as such it is "a satchel bomb packed with high explosives." That language seemed hyperbolic to me, although I had to admit that I had rarely found a book so compelling—certainly never one about Bible study.

Every morning after the boys left for school, I sat in the quiet kitchen and read a chapter and worked alone through the exercises intended for a group. One frequent directive was to imagine being each character in a biblical story—a way to live in the story. For the first time in my life, these familiar stories became three-dimensional. They moved off of the boring brown landscape I had assigned them in childhood and became living, vibrant incidents in which I could insert myself. I could participate in the complex life they held. "I find [this book] exciting," I wrote in my journal. "I know I want to study Carl Jung, and I want to learn much more about the Bible as well."

One morning the exercises included using clay to express what might be going on internally at an unconscious level. I had no clay, so I pulled out the playdough recipe I used for Jeremy and made a batch. A small, empty bowl—or was it a nest?—emerged from my fingers. What was I, empty or pregnant? Could I be both? Empty of ideas? Full of potential? I wanted to be full. I was tired of feeling empty, of wondering, but my fingers did not know how to fill it. I placed my emptiness on the windowsill where I could ponder it each day as I prepared dinner or washed dishes.

ॐ

After a second seminary extension class, I knew with certainty that I wanted to go to seminary. A family friend suggested that the Episcopal seminary in Alexandria might be a good fit for me. That sounded both daunting and intriguing—"a breath of fresh air," I wrote in my journal. However, Episcopalians felt so far from my world that it seemed bold even to knock on their door. I had to talk myself into calling Virginia Theological Seminary to request a catalog and then to follow up by making an appointment with the registrar.

The campus itself literally felt like "a breath of fresh air" after my nerve-wracking drive on the Capital Beltway, which I had always made a point to avoid. Here was a peaceful oasis, an open, grassy sweep of lawn surrounded by giant oak trees that offered shade on this early summer afternoon. Brick buildings clustered around the edge of the lawn. One old building with a cupola and uniquely shaped windows seemed to preside over the campus, and a chapel with stained glass windows sat off to the side.

In my interview, I learned that I could begin taking classes part-time, but I would need to wait to go through an evaluation process to be admitted into the Master of Divinity program. That was OK with me because I still felt tentative.

I returned home knowing I now needed to face the real possibility of returning to school. I rehashed all my uncertainties. I looked around at my beloved house, where I felt comfortable and safe. If I went to school,

I would have to be gone a lot and would have less time for some of the things I most enjoyed. I thought of our house filled with the aroma of baking bread, of clean sheets scented by fresh outside air. Would I have time for baking or hanging laundry on the clothesline? I wandered out to stand under our oak tree and look at my flower beds. Bright zinnias and marigolds waved in the breeze. Bees hovered over rosemary, and white cabbage moths flitted around. I probably wouldn't have time to leisurely pick flowers in the early morning, walking through still-wet grass as the sun melted away the shadows. Instead, I'd be rushing off to school.

If I were gone for parts of many days, I'd have to consolidate house-work, and evenings would be for studying. Assignments, deadlines, and tests would drive my schedule. It would be much less complicated, much easier, to stay at home and continue to cook, clean, and go on field trips with my sons—Wayne thought that was the only sensible solution. No seminary arrangement could be a good one from his perspective. Be-sides, what would I do with a seminary degree, he asked? I had no answer, just a burning desire to go.

The only problem with the simple or sensible solution was that I knew it wouldn't work. I had glimpsed something more and wouldn't be satisfied with my old routines. I wanted Wayne's support, but I knew that my decision could not rest on his preferences. I kept waffling. Shirley encouraged me to move ahead, and Wil told me that, in his experience, a person needs to follow urges when they come because often, if you wait, the urge may dissipate, leaving you with nothing but regret.

Finally, in mid-July I sent in my application, and the waffling stopped. I began to focus on which classes would fit my middle-of-the-day window of availability, how I would get the boys off in the morning, and what to do on days they were sick or had no school. Wayne contin-ued to be uncertain and fearful of the change. He had grown used to me being at home to keep everything running smoothly and was afraid of what might be expected of him in this new arrangement. He declared, "I want you to know that I am not going to be coming home and making supper for the boys."

On that note, my new venture began.

32

Metanoia

THE CAR AHEAD OF me skidded and slid into the first traffic lane as I approached the on-ramp to I-66. I was on the way to my first day of seminary. My heart pounded, and my hands felt clammy. Would I skid too? Was I sliding into dangerous territory, into a new and foreign land? Fortunately, the car ahead of me was not hit, nor did I skid. I merged smoothly into the flow of fast-moving vehicles.

Once on campus, I found my way to a classroom in Aspinwall, the building with the white cupola and fancy windows. There I joined a group of complete strangers. They had attended several beginning-of-the-year events in which I hadn't been included because of my part-time status, but even so, everyone felt the newness of this venture. All the seats in the back of the room were taken, so I made my way to an open one on the front row and introduced myself to the woman beside me. Her name was Sherry. She lived in Springfield and was also a day student. She told me she liked sitting at the front of the room, and I acknowledged that I did too. Tony, our professor, welcomed us, introduced himself, and laid out the guidelines and requirements for the course. Was I up to this, I wondered? Others probably felt the same, even though no one showed it on their face. At the end of the first week of school I wrote, "It's been both a stressful and exciting week. At moments I feel exhilarated . . . and at others wonder what in the world I think I am doing."

I had always thought of Episcopalians as upper-class, sophisticated people who lived in a rarified world of high church pomp and ceremony. Mennonites were at the other end of the spectrum, having little ritual and even less sense of how to conduct themselves in the world of stained-glass windows, vestments, kneeling, and standing. I soon learned that most of my stereotypes did not hold. Episcopalians were comfortable with liturgy that felt strange and complex to me, but they were not necessarily wealthy or sophisticated. They had the same interests and fears I did. We were more alike than different. The stories of how we had gotten to seminary held many commonalities.

Nevertheless, I battled with my timidity. Each day I arrived on campus, went directly to my classes, and headed home afterward as quickly as I could. I saw others heading to the refectory while I sat alone at a picnic table eating my brown bag lunch. I went to the library, found what I needed, and left as quickly as possible. I didn't attend chapel.

After a week or so of "hiding," I realized that I needed to venture farther afield. That was triggered by a classmate inviting me to have lunch with her in the refectory. I went and discovered it was easy to navigate. I could even bring my packed lunch if I liked and eat with others. After that I decided I needed to assign myself one new place to explore each day until I became familiar with the entire campus. One day I attended midday prayers at the chapel. Another day I explored the library, checking out each floor and finding the study carrels, the special collections, and the periodicals. Another day I spent time in the bookstore rather than dashing in simply to buy a required text book.

I loved my classes and could hardly believe I was doing this thing I wanted to do. Even so, I hesitated to acknowledge that *I* had made a significant decision. I wrote in my journal, "I feel overwhelmed by the goodness of all that is happening to me."

༄

Second semester brought homiletics class. I felt my usual trepidation as I contemplated preaching—uncertain about standing in the raised pulpit and projecting my voice out over a congregation. Yet the dynamics of writing sermons fascinated me. Unlike essays, sermons were a hybrid of written and oral work with a structure all their own. I found it a compelling process, at least until I tried it. Every sermon needed to contain good news, said Milton, our homiletics professor, and good news was not conditional, not followed by an *if*. Identifying good news was more challenging than any of us thought.

My first sermon felt wooden, the second only a little less so. The third, no one could connect with. The fourth and final one loomed before me. The texts were Jesus' parable of the talents and Romans 12, verses about being transformed because of God's mercy.

I struggled with the transformation theme, not sure where to find good news. Everything I thought to say sounded self-righteous or judgmental and full of conditions. The Gospel parable was about a man giving his servants talents (coins) to invest: to one he gave five, to another two, and to a third he gave one. The servants given five and two talents invested them and earned more money for their master. The third buried his single talent because he was afraid he couldn't invest it profitably, and thus he incurred his master's wrath. I couldn't find much good news here either, especially for the servant who buried his talent. That two people had been given more than the other represented the usual unfairness of life as I saw it. I was clearly a "one talent" person—talent refers to a coin, but in this story, *talent* is often used to mean ability.

The more I dithered, the more impossible the task became. I could think of no way to use Jesus' parable. I busied myself with a term paper I needed to finish. I cleaned the house. I attended a daylong conference on pastoral care for people with disabilities. The presenter had been born with no arms, and he talked about the process of learning to dig deep within himself to find the resources for meeting the challenges life brought him. I was quite sure I had no inside reserve deep enough to meet the requirements for this sermon.

My turn to preach in class came every three weeks and was now fast approaching. It was Monday afternoon and the class met on Wednesday. I sat down at my big oak desk that had belonged to Grandpa, wishing that some of his wisdom would seep out of the grains in its golden wood and into me. I couldn't give up. I was too responsible, too compelled to finish what I began, but this was an impossible trap. I identified with the servant given the single talent: life wasn't fair for him; it wasn't fair for me either. I angrily took up my pen and wrote, "I am burying my talent. I can't do this." I imagined standing next to a bush with a garden shovel in hand, digging a hole much larger than needed for one small piece of money, and hurling in my shiny coin. I imagined piling the dirt high on top of it. Then I got up from my desk and washed the lunch dishes. I came back. The mound of fresh dirt was still there, like a wound, partly hidden by the bush. I didn't know how to attend to it, so I went out to check the wash hanging on the line to see if it was dry. I came back to my desk. I sat down and looked at my paper again. I began writing about how I couldn't do this. I described the successful sermon my classmate Bob had preached about Jesus riding into Jerusalem on a donkey. I wrote about the tidy, well-constructed sermon another classmate Mary had given, saying that I simply couldn't do what she had done. I sat there some more. I muttered. I wanted to skip class, to go away and not come back for a long time. I was completely empty. I had no words.

But I simply couldn't walk away. I hovered, not sure whether to scream or give up. Instead, I grabbed my imaginary shovel and dug down into the dirt and found the coin again. I sat at my desk envisioning the now grubby coin in my hand. It looked tarnished and ill-used. What could I do with it? It had been given me and was mine to use. As I sat there immobilized, my anger began to slip away. In its place came a realization that I was loved beyond measure, loved fully and completely without a breath of the judgment I heaped on myself. This love contained the mercy the apostle Paul cited in Romans 12 as the basis for offering ourselves to God to be transformed. God's mercy saw me as a fully able preacher, no matter what grade my professor would give me, no matter how humble my sermons were compared to those of my classmates. My coin might be grubby, but it was what I had to use. God had given it to me and had called me to use it. That had to be enough.

I began writing again, this time not angrily but with deep gratitude. I wrote about my talent, my despair in trying to use it, my envy of others' sermons and the many bright talents they represented. I described digging a hole under the bush and burying my coin. The words seemed to flow. I wrote about digging through the dirt of my envy, anger, and imagined helplessness and finding the coin again. I wrote about realizing that no matter how grubby and insignificant it appeared, it was what I had been given to use. I described my sense of God's love and mercy, my realization that who I was was enough—that I could offer what I had because of a mercy that surrounded me with love and created good, even out of attempts that appeared less-than-adequate to me.

It seemed a shabby little sermon, a personal story of struggle, anger, despair, and then mercy and love. But it would have to do. I had no time to try something else. I read it to Sherry on Wednesday and she made a few suggestions. Then it was class time.

When I stepped up into the elevated pulpit in the chapel to begin, I felt at peace. I glanced around the chapel, lit only by the filtered light coming through stained glass windows. My half dozen classmates sat scattered in the pews before me.

I took a breath. "This week I buried my talent," I began. "I had a sermon to write and I couldn't write it." The class members gave startled laughs. Was this a joke? This wasn't how a sermon on the parable of the talents usually began. I should have been talking about the virtues of *not* burying a talent. Instead, I recounted my struggle with writing, my envy of others' sermons, and my anger. I described burying the talent under a bush and piling high the dirt, but then not being able to walk away from it. I told about digging it up again. Everyone listened. No one looked bored. They were with me. I spoke about sitting with my grimy coin and, in contrast to my own judgment, feeling surrounded by God's mercy and love. My one coin was enough. I didn't need to preach like anyone else. I could offer the talent I had. That was all God asked of me. I was loved as I was. God was merciful to me even when I resisted. God was merciful to us all.

I slowly gathered my notes and went down the steps. By the time I got to the bottom, Bob was there to give me a big hug. He took my arm and almost danced me out of the chapel, back to our classroom. Robbin was crying. Mary was teary. Everyone was moved.

Milton handed out the evaluation sheets we filled in after each sermon, and the room became quiet as everyone wrote. Then Bob shoved his evaluation paper over to me. "Metanoia strikes again!!!" he had written in bold letters across the bottom. *Metanoia* is a Greek word that means to turn around, to go in a different direction. The week before, he had spoken about metanoia in his sermon, and while I hadn't mentioned it, clearly it had happened for me this week.

I looked around the room. Robbin continued to cry and Mary wiped her eyes. I was mostly in shock. I had been unprepared for this. Milton turned to me and asked how I felt about the sermon. "I'm afraid it was more Jungian than theological," I apologized, "and too personal."

"Jungian and theological meet sometimes," he replied. "And you found a way to take something personal and make it about all of us." I hadn't known I was doing that, but people's responses made it clear that my message had reached into their hearts.

I knew what I had done was bigger than me, but exactly what or how I couldn't say. Clearly, God was present in what had happened, but God wouldn't be sitting at Grandpa's desk, writing my sermons for me. I'd have to do that. Was this a fluke—finding the right words at the right time? Could I trust that I might be able to preach a good sermon again? I was glad it had been my last one for the semester. Another homiletics class was coming in my senior year, but that was a long way off. I could relax for the present.

⚬⊚⚬

Wayne and I continued to grapple with my changing life. An opportunity came up for me to participate in a weekend of nonviolence training that would require me to go to D.C. several days in a row. Wayne was concerned about my driving there alone and what this training might lead to. I told him about it at supper, and we discussed it briefly. He was not in favor, but I wasn't ready to give it up.

When we went to bed that night, I could tell he was unhappy. I crawled in beside him, turned out my light, and lay there in the tense silence.

"What are you thinking?" I finally asked. Silence. "I know you don't like the idea of me going to this class." More silence.

After a bit, he turned toward me, thumping his pillow into shape and said, "I don't like it. When will you ever stop? You keep pushing and pushing and expect me just to go along with whatever you do. Next, you'll want to go to demonstrations, and that could be dangerous. You aren't thinking about us. Do we even matter anymore?"

"Of course you matter," I replied. "That's why I am talking about it. I think the class sounds interesting, but I'm not positive I want to go."

"I don't think you should," he said. "You're already in school. Isn't that enough? It feels like we are growing further and further apart, and I don't see how our marriage will survive if you keep doing this."

I knew Wayne was uncomfortable and scared, but I had never seriously considered that our marriage might not survive. I had always assumed Wayne would be there, even if he wasn't always completely happy. In spite of this new concern, I had a moment of clarity that surprised me.

"I can't go backward and be my old self again," I said. "All I know is that I have begun to change and grow and I can't stop it. I hope you will be a part of it because I want us to grow together." Silence again. I lay only inches away from Wayne, but it felt like miles. I looked at the small panes of the dormer window beyond the foot of our bed and wondered what would happen to us. Would this night mark the point from which I went on without Wayne, or would his fear subside so that he too could grow? I wasn't sure.

In the end, I decided not to attend the class. I had too many things to do already and, besides, even though I was interested, I didn't see myself as a demonstrator—I wasn't as fearless as Wayne thought I was. All the same, I knew other opportunities might come up that would bring us to this same point again.

I was right. Another decision point presented itself with the new school year. I had finished two years of part-time work and was now a full-time student. This included a field placement: twelve hours a week of working in a congregation as a pastoral assistant. I would be preaching, teaching, visiting parishioners, doing administrative chores, and helping with other pastoral duties. No one was allowed to serve in their home church, so I made arrangements to work at the Manassas Church of the Brethren, a denomination that holds beliefs similar to Mennonites'.

Once again, school reached into my family's life, calling into question where they would attend church. Wayne was still tentative about seeing me in visible leadership roles, but he didn't like the idea of us attending different churches. Should he and the boys remain at our Mennonite congregation, or should they come with me to the Church of the Brethren? I was happy when he decided to join me.

The church welcomed and supported us all. Even though my public speaking was sometimes awkward, the respect and encouragement I received helped Wayne to slowly become more comfortable with my role. One Sunday after I had preached, I asked him to drop off a book at a member's home. When he told me what happened, I knew he had turned a corner.

The family had parents visiting that week, and the visiting woman answered his knock. She looked at him and said, "Oh, you're the preacher's wife." Wayne laughed as he told me about it and added that he hadn't bothered to correct her.

33

The Grief I Didn't Know Was There

My FINAL YEAR OF seminary was filled with classes, papers, fieldwork, housework, and family responsibilities. I managed to hold all the parts of my life together, but I felt perpetually overwhelmed and resented any unexpected demand on my time. I knew I was barely hanging on, so I asked my pastoral care professor for a recommendation for a therapist. He sent me to a large pastoral counseling organization where I was assigned to a therapist named Becky.

"I feel like I'm carrying a heavy backpack that I can't put down," I said in my first session. Over the next weeks, Becky asked me many questions, which I thought I answered well. I understood my life; I could explain its ins and outs, its contradictions and anomalies. I hoped she might say that I had good insight into myself, that there was really nothing I needed to work on. But she didn't. Instead, she listened to what I said—and to what I didn't say. I foolishly wondered to myself if many of her clients understood themselves as well as I did, but I kept returning. Having someone to listen to me satisfied a longing I hadn't been fully aware of.

Some months into therapy she asked a question no one had ever asked me, one I never would have thought to ask myself. I mentioned casually that the anniversary of my father's death was coming and that I had talked to my sisters about getting flowers for Mother to mark the occasion. "Who is getting flowers for you?" she asked. I looked at her, taken aback. I fumbled for an answer. Why did *I* need flowers? My sisters and I had done this for years. It was a thoughtful thing to do. Why would she question it? She spoke again, more softly than before, saying, "Who gets flowers for you? This was your loss too." She paused, then continued, "Your mother could get another husband, but you can never get another father."

Tears filled my eyes. My throat constricted. I had nothing to say. I remembered telling Becky without any particular emotion about the night Papa died, how I sat rocking and rocking. Becky guessed what I was thinking. Into the silence between us she offered only a few more words, "I think you've found that little girl rocking in her chair again."

Over the next months, I unearthed deep wells of tears I had no idea still existed, grief that leaked energy from my life, along with anger at my father's death. It lay hidden under my need to be perfect and in control, buried by my unconscious drive to prevent such a thing from happening again. I thought my grief had been acknowledged and left behind, but I found it was still present. I became aware of the energy it required to keep it locked away. I learned that memories were more than the stories I could tell; they were also the tears and emotions that came unbidden at surprising moments, once I gave them permission to come. I asked my mother if I had cried much after Papa's death and she said, "No, you never did." I'm shedding those tears now, I thought to myself.

New memories came back to me, memories of the many times people sympathized with my mother. I would be standing beside her, but no one addressed me. Instead, they commented that she must be glad to have three daughters to comfort her. Neither my loss nor my grief was named. I imagine those well-meaning people had no idea of how to address a child of three or four about her grief. I was young and resilient, they must have thought, so I would get over this. But I heard and took in what they said. I was there to comfort mother—the loss was hers. At home we talked about how we all missed Papa, but even there my own feelings were not singled out as important. The grief belonged to us all.

Now, for the first time, my loss was being peeled off from the family tragedy, from Mother's grief, from that of my sisters, who each had their own experience, and I felt almost as bereft as if Papa had just died. I didn't like this process. My adult togetherness was shattered. I couldn't focus. I felt vulnerabilities I didn't know I had. I also felt anger. Why had this happened to me so many years ago, and why did it still need to haunt my life? Why couldn't I just move beyond it? I began to learn the reality that grief never leaves and that the only way to incorporate it into one's life is to allow oneself to experience it. I needed to go through it, to learn its lessons, and to accept the new depths it created. Working with Becky opened me in ways I had not thought possible.

❦

My therapy did not focus only on grief. This was my senior year and homiletics had come into my life again. I still struggled with it—not as severely as I had in the first class, but enough to make me anxious. I spent many counseling sessions talking about my fears.

The "little girl at the mic," as I called her, came back into my life. At some point, I told Becky about the time I confidently asked to speak into my father's mic, and how my voice had faded away to nothing when he held it out to me. That timid little girl who was perpetually afraid to give voice to herself seemed to perch on my shoulder, warning me of the dangers, imagined or real, that I faced by being assertive. I became aware of the many ways I retreated into the "safety" of silence—a safety that carried a high price in terms of the anger, pain, and fear I suppressed. I wrote out dialogues between her and my adult self, acknowledging those fears, reassuring her, and reminding her that I was now capable of being clear and articulate. I had an adult voice that could be trusted; she could stop being fearful. Change inched into my life.

I had a different teacher for Homiletics II: Callie, who made me want to preach. She talked about the art and craft of sermons as well as the content. We talked about the need for scripture to become alive to us before we could bring it to life for others and about prayer and silence as necessary ingredients. We talked about poetry. I listened eagerly, but when it was my turn to preach, I could not write the sermons I felt inside, nor could I deliver them convincingly. My classmates said I didn't speak loudly enough.

One day Callie asked me to stay after class to work on voice projection. Before we began, I told her how much I was enjoying the class even though I said little in discussions. "You don't need to say much," she replied. "You have expressive eyes. I can see you sitting here, drinking everything in." No one had ever said such a thing to me before.

There was a moment of silence. Then Callie spoke again. "Let me tell you what your strength is as a preacher." Another pause. "Give me your hands," she said, holding hers out to me, "and look into my eyes." I placed my hands in hers and stood looking at her. She spoke slowly, clearly, emphatically: "Kathie, you have a deep desire to share your faith with others. It's evidence of God touching your life in a personal way. No amount of practice or work could ever achieve that, and no one can take it away from you. The things you are concerned about are small and easily fixed."

My eyes filled with tears. Callie had graced me with a blessing in the middle of an ordinary school day. I stood in Key Hall, where our class met, aware of nothing but her words and the sun shining brightly through the open door behind us. I tried to take in what she had said, but I had no response other than my tears.

When she released my hands, I went to the pulpit and spoke to her as she stood in the back of the room. I had no difficulty in projecting my voice. My anxiety, not my voice, was the problem. That was something I could work on.

34

Graduation

I PULLED INTO THE parking space at the side of our house and switched off the engine, home from Alexandria for another day, except this wasn't just another day. It was the last day of school. How many times had I made this trip, I wondered? It had often felt like seminary would never be finished, that the days were too many to count. Then I'd have to stop looking ahead and pull myself back to the present to deal with the coming day. Projecting into the future overwhelmed me. But, like the grains of sand in an hourglass, the days had dropped singly, one after another, and now they were all spent. Finishing didn't feel quite as triumphant as I thought it would.

In spite of my resistance to school, I had come to enjoy many aspects of it. I had made good friends. I had gained confidence and discovered new parts of myself. But I was also glad to be free, to have no more papers or exams. No more evaluations. Today, I had turned in my final exam and picked up the last notices about graduation events from my mail slot in Meade Hall.

Instead of feeling jubilant and heading home, I had found myself reluctant to leave the now deserted campus. I sat down on a bench in the afternoon sun, wanting to linger, to hold on to the moment and savor it. I looked over the green lawn to the old oak trees. Aspinwall Hall, with its tall, narrow windows and white cupola, presided over the circular drive as it had for more than a century. Other buildings seemed to have retreated into the shade, except for Sparrow Hall reclining in the sun like a sleeping cat. The only sounds were muffled traffic and a few birds braving the afternoon heat.

Graduation day at Virginia Theological Seminary.

I had spent more days here than I could count and knew the campus well. I had just turned in the key to the day-student lounge I opened every morning when I arrived at seven o'clock, ahead of rush hour traffic. I'd seen the names of soldiers scrawled in Aspinwall's tower, where they had been held captive when the school served as a military hospital during the Civil War. I had spent a small fortune at the photocopier in the library, had my customary seat for morning chapel, and knew which condiments I liked to add to my lunch salad in the refectory. I had been in only a few faculty homes, but I knew who lived in each house scattered around the periphery of the campus, and I knew which parking lots were likely to have spaces at different times of the day.

In my years here, I had come to feel connected to the Episcopal world in a way that enriched me. I liked the liturgy, the carefully and artfully chosen words used in worship, the contemplative emphasis that had been missing in my own upbringing, and the sense of sacramental living that my practical Anabaptist world was not quick to cultivate. I had not given up my tradition, but my faith had been enlarged and enriched.

I had grown to love this school that had once so intimidated me. It had become a part of me, just as I felt a part of it, but it would no longer be "mine" in the same way. Classmates would scatter. Professors would change, and I would never again participate in its daily activities. A life-changing segment of my life was over. I surprised myself by being nearer to tears than rejoicing.

❧

On Monday morning, I headed out early for graduation. The sky was a clear blue and trees held the first intense green of summer. I didn't need even a light jacket on the fresh May morning as I directed guests to a secondary parking lot across the street from the seminary.

Mother and Jeanie came from Harrisonburg. Geoffrey and Jeremy, off from school for the day, arrived with Wayne. He surveyed me in my borrowed cassock and surplice and smiled broadly. I smiled to myself, remembering how fearful he had been about me coming here. He had come a long way, just as I had. He had even made supper for the boys on more than one occasion, I mused, thinking of his long-ago ultimatum of which he now conveniently had no memory.

I showed my family their seats on the lawn facing the yellow and white canopy where the ceremony would take place. Then I went to join my classmates who were lining up to process in. Each of us wore a cross made from one of the oak trees on campus that had had to be taken down. Like the tree that was once whole, we had also been a unit, studying and worshiping together, arguing, laughing, crying, supporting each other. Now, wherever we went, we would carry with us this small piece of Virginia Theological Seminary as a reminder of the whole from which we came—that, in addition to all the usual symbolism of a cross.

After the speeches and conferral of honorary degrees, our turn finally came. The dean began handing out diplomas. I saw Jeanie getting her camera ready as he moved through the list of seniors toward the names starting with *J* and *K*. She stepped into the aisle for a better vantage point, but my name wasn't called. She looked confused as the *L*s began, consulted her program, and sat down again.

Then the degrees with honors were named, and I stood up. She and Mother smiled with surprise and pride. Wayne looked equally pleased, although he had known in advance. I was doing what none of us had considered, graduating cum laude. It was so beyond my thinking that I had never even bothered to say I couldn't do it. I smiled at that irony and allowed myself to bask in my success.

35

Counselor

Most of my classmates were poised to begin new jobs, but I had no work prospects. My few leads led to dead ends. None of the Mennonite churches within commuting distance that were looking for a pastor wanted a woman. Wayne was in the middle of a major building project at work and didn't want to relocate, and besides, after our move to Manassas in the middle of Geoffrey's elementary years, we had promised we wouldn't disrupt his high school. The only thing I could look forward to was a part-time counseling course that would begin in the fall.

Back in February, well before graduation, my good friend Sherry and I met at a bagel place in a nondescript strip mall, a rare treat for us. As we sat spreading cream cheese on our bagels and sipping coffee, our conversation turned to what I might be doing a year from then. She was in her first pastoral position, having graduated the year before. (Since I had begun as a part-time student, it took me four years to complete the three-year program.) I was looking for a church to pastor but was coming up with nothing. "Did you know that PC&CC has a training course for pastors who want to improve their counseling skills?" Sherry asked me, referring to the Pastoral Counseling and Consultation Centers, where Becky worked. I knew Becky helped in a counselor training program, but I had not heard about the pastors' training division. I said I'd ask her about it. The idea sounded appealing, but I was still holding out for a position in a church.

The next week when I asked Becky, she not only confirmed what Sherry had said but encouraged me to apply. It sounded like a good backup plan if nothing else materialized. I sent in an application but continued looking for a church position. In early June I learned that I was accepted into the center's Institute for Pastoral Psychotherapy (IPP). The downside was that I'd need to find a new counselor because Becky would become one of my teachers.

No other pastoral position became available. That is how I found myself driving to Oakton on a bright, clear September morning for the first day of classes in the IPP. The challenge that morning was finding the designated parking lot for interns several blocks from the administrative offices and classrooms. Another woman was getting out of a car as I pulled in, and she introduced herself to me: Karen, who was in her third year of the program. As we walked down the sidewalk, she chatted away, putting me at ease.

We entered the building and I followed her to the meeting room, where we took seats at two large tables that were pushed together, filling most of the space. John, the director, welcomed us. As part of his introduction, he commented that the two-year clergy track had just been eliminated. *What?* I thought to myself. He hadn't bothered to tell me that in our interview. I glanced around the room, but no one else appeared surprised or even fazed by that. I said nothing, feeling much too shy to assert myself in front of these strangers. John went on to explain that the special track was essentially the first two years of the longer, pastoral counseling course, so parish clergy could opt for two of the three years. I still felt blindsided.

John asked us to introduce ourselves, and the third-year students, all younger than I was, jumped right in, entertaining us with vivid details about their past experiences and present goals. First- and second-year students talked, but I kept hesitating, awed by the competence of everyone else. Finally, I was the only one who hadn't spoken and there were only ten minutes left. I felt slighted—John should have monitored the time better. Yet, on the other hand, I was relieved not to have to reveal much of my lackluster experience. I had been going through the litany of my deficiencies in my mind: I was the only one in the group who had never pastored a church. I didn't have any experience in counseling. I was a recent seminary graduate who couldn't find a job, a forty-four-year-old woman who had stayed home with her children. Was there any way I could fit in here?

That evening I took my sons to their orchestra rehearsal at a school on the other side of the county. While they practiced, I sat in a deserted, windowless hallway, surrounded by the cacophony of several groups

rehearsing different parts in separate rooms. I read through all the materials I had been given about the IPP program, and the more I read,
the more overwhelmed I became. I couldn't possibly accomplish what
would be expected of me. How was it that Becky thought I'd do well in
this program? I felt numb once again. I could not picture myself interacting with the strong, confident third-year women. I couldn't stand up for
myself at all—I hadn't even been able to express my surprise at John's
announcement about dropping the parish clergy track. I should call him
and tell him I needed to withdraw, that this program wasn't right for me.
Yet I had wanted badly to be accepted. When I heard about the program,
I had thought it sounded good and matched my interests. I had no other
job to turn to. How could I explain why I was quitting?

By morning, my anxiety had begun to recede and when classes
started the following week, I felt more comfortable. The third-year
women and the men in my class continued to intimidate me. They talked
about themselves with ease and challenged others seemingly without effort. They took up lots of class time while I pulled back in awe, allowing
them to do so. The person with whom I felt the most kinship was Darnell,
one of the two African American men in my class. Even though he drove
a "Benz" and was termed a "clotheshorse" by the other women, he was
warm and personable and down-to-earth. He admitted to me that he too
had not been told about IPP dropping the parish clergy track, nor had he
had the courage to say anything.

Within weeks of starting the program we began to see clients. I was
probably more uneasy than my first client was. But at least she had never
seen a therapist, so she couldn't compare me to someone else. My second
client, a young man who had been dismissed from his job, was full of
anger. After he had talked at length, I observed that he sounded angry.
I almost added, "You really ought to see a therapist," but caught myself
in time, startled by the realization that this is exactly what he was doing.
I was it. I couldn't pass him on to some wise person who would know
exactly what to do.

During the second semester, one of the third-year women decided
to apply for membership in the American Association of Pastoral Counselors (AAPC) and was given an interview at their spring meeting. She
spoke about her preparation: the case study she needed to present based
on a taped session with a client and an extensive reflection paper on herself as a pastoral counselor. I was relieved that I wasn't going to become a

pastoral counselor because I couldn't imagine myself doing all that. Even so, I knew I wanted to complete the three-year program.

If seminary had felt like coming home to myself, this program seemed like discovering the room in the house where I most wanted to spend my time. Pastoral counseling flowed seamlessly out of theology. While it was similar to other counseling in that we studied various counseling theories, normal and abnormal development, marriage and family counseling, group therapy, and career counseling, there was more. We were learning to be *pastoral* counselors, and we talked about the intersection of theology and psychology: how to "translate" those two languages to each other, the places they met, and where they diverged. We studied faith development and assessment. We paid attention to our own spiritual life and development and to ways of making space for the holy in our work. Our goal was not to proselytize but to support clients in using their own faith experiences as an integral part of change and healing. While many counselors are not allowed to speak of religious or spiritual matters, as pastoral counselors, we were able to do so.

Becky recommended Rosamond to me as a new therapist, and with her a new phase of my therapy began. Rosamond helped me to move out from my past. She suggested a metaphor for my work: pushing out the walls of the chapel at Eastern Mennonite College (now University). I had told her about Grandpa's memorial service there, when many people came to speak with other family members, but no one sought me out. And I talked about more recent times when I felt like I was on the sidelines, if not completely invisible. Yet that campus chapel was a place central to my life. I had childhood memories of the building: fidgeting through church services and choir programs on its hard wooden benches, playing with Aunt Esther's teacher's aids in a basement classroom, and attending children's meetings in the room where I pondered the painting of Dirk Willems pulling his pursuer out of the icy river. I sat in the auditorium through innumerable high school and college chapel services and classes, stood on the stage for choir rehearsals and programs, and even dusted the benches with a long-handled mop as part of a summer cleaning job. It was where I'd seen Wayne waiting to ask me for our first date, and it was where my parents were married and where Papa's funeral had taken place.

The chapel, now named for Grandpa, represented the heart of my life in a way few other places did, and it also represented my current experience of feeling unknown and in the background. Rosamond said I needed to push out those four walls. What had once brought me security now felt limiting, and I needed to begin to inhabit a larger world in which I could function and be noticed and known for myself. Yet even hearing her say that made my heart skip a beat. As much as I wanted it, being noticed felt intimidating. I wasn't sure I wanted to be the focus of others' attention.

Rosamond suggested beginning with a small change, something easy, like clothing. I bought a pair of slim black stretch pants, a style popular at the time, and wore them to our next session. They were more form-fitting than any I had ever worn and out of character with my image of myself. I felt awkward and uncomfortable when she enthused over them, but I loved wearing something a little daring—at least for me.

Rosamond and I also talked about my anger and how to use it constructively, not just softening it into tears. With its hard edge I could push ahead and face new challenges. I could push out the chapel walls and make a place for myself in the world. Becky had told me similar things, and I knew them in my head, but now I began to incorporate them into my life.

Year two of the internship brought me more confidence. With the group of third-year women gone and a new class below me, there was more space in which I could expand, but I was still guarded. Several of the men in the program had enrolled in a concomitant program at Garrett-Evangelical Theological Seminary through which they would earn a doctor of ministry degree in pastoral counseling. Even saying all that was a mouthful. They talked about their seminars in Evanston, Illinois, all the books they were reading, and the papers they had to write. I had not been aware of that program, but it didn't sound like anything I'd want to do— too academic and theoretical. I didn't want to do any more schooling. I listened quietly, grateful that I didn't need to follow them there.

However, working as a counselor captivated and energized me. When the door of my counseling room closed and I was sitting there with one or two people, I felt like a new world was about to open between us. Some clients came with stories that flowed out in orderly fashion. Others presented a jumble that was indicative of the jumble of their lives. There were yet others who revealed things bit by bit, either because we needed to build trust first or because there were stories and details they had hidden, even from themselves. I felt privileged to enter intimate spaces of others' lives and to witness their pain, their courage, and their hard work to move toward health.

During my third year, I embarked on one of the things I'd told myself I'd never do: I applied to become a member of the American Association of Pastoral Counselors. Now I was the one recording a session and writing about it and myself. When I passed my interview and became a member, I felt relief. I wouldn't have to move beyond member level. That was enough for me. I was now forty-six years old and finally ready to begin a new career.

One Sunday afternoon late in the spring of 1993, I graduated from the IPP. The next Sunday I was ordained at Northern Virginia Mennonite Church (now Daniels Run Peace Church). It was a joyous occasion graced with the attendance of fellow interns, seminary classmates, family, and friends. Geoffrey had returned from college just in time to be there, and Mother and Jeanie came. There were well-chosen words and good music but much less formality and pomp than at the ordinations of my Episcopal friends. I had hoped that a church position would come along with ordination, but that wasn't going to happen. For the time being, my pastoral work would be as a counselor.

Though I felt that I had bungled some responses at my interview for a position at Pastoral Counseling and Consultation Centers, I was hired and started a few weeks after my ordination. No more hoops to jump through—from now on I would learn as I worked. I was heading toward the far side of middle age and wanted to be settled and established.

Through all this work, I had inadvertently brought myself to a new decision point. Did I want to look for a church to pastor, or did I want to continue working as a pastoral counselor? Maybe I could combine the two. About a year after joining the PC&CC staff, I was asked to serve part-time as interim pastor at Oakton Church of the Brethren. That fit well because I was still in the process of building a caseload. However, when the interim position ended, I knew I didn't want to feel constantly pulled in two directions. I needed to choose between pastoring a church and being a pastoral counselor. I chose the counseling. I already had a job in that field, whereas finding a church was an uncertain prospect at best. I grieved the loss of my original dream, but I was ready to be settled.

At some point I had read *A Severe Mercy* by Sheldon Vanauken, a book that contained letters written by C. S. Lewis to him and his wife. In one letter Lewis commented that "perpetual spring-time" is not allowed, meaning that the couple couldn't live forever in the first blush of being in love. Had Lewis been writing to me he would have paraphrased his advice by saying that "perpetual coasting" is not allowed.

I wouldn't have wanted to hear that any more than the lovestruck couple in the book wanted to acknowledge Lewis's comment to them. I hoped against hope that coasting was allowed, that I would have no more hoops to jump through, that I was done meeting requirements. I had taken enough risks. I wanted to sit back and enjoy how far I had come. I wanted to coast.

36

Demon

WAYNE AND I SAT eating dinner on a perfect summer evening, the smell of freshly cut grass coming through an open window and fronds of the Boston fern moving gently in the breeze. We could hear the splashing of the fountain in the park across the street. Inside, my favorite Schubert lieder were playing—songs I had learned from Grandpa's records. They carried with them the misty nostalgia of childhood and safety. Usually I enjoyed this music, but now I was near tears.

Tomorrow I'd fly to Chicago alone. I'd take a taxi to the apartment where I would be house-sitting, use the owners' unfamiliar car to find my way to Evanston, and meet my new classmates and professors at Garrett-Evangelical Theological Seminary. I was about to begin the doctor of ministry program I had once dismissed as something I'd never do. Here at home in Virginia, my flower beds were at their peak and we were having fresh radishes and beans from the garden.

My mind, once again, went through the reasoning that got me here, hoping to find an escape. After my interim pastoral position, I knew that if I wanted to continue as a pastoral counselor, I needed to be licensed. Otherwise, I would be limited in where I could work, and I hadn't come this far to find myself stuck, unable to move or change jobs. Licensure required a graduate degree in counseling, and my seminary degree lacked enough counseling hours to qualify. Either I could get a second master's degree in counseling—and retake most of the classes I had already taken in the IPP—or I could enroll in the distance learning program at Garrett. I had chosen the latter. Geoffrey and Jeremy were gone now, so my being away for three-week blocks of time wasn't a problem where they were concerned.

I desperately didn't want to go to school again. I didn't want to write papers and wade through hours of dense reading. I didn't want to be away from home, where Schubert lieder were playing and the evening was taking on a golden glow, but I saw no other route.

The next day Wayne took me to the airport. I cried when I hugged him goodbye, and I dabbed stray tears on the plane, hoping my seatmate wouldn't notice. By the time the flight arrived, I had pulled myself together. I acted adult as I picked up my luggage, got a cab, and followed the instructions I had been given to where I'd be staying.

I explored the apartment, which at any other time I would have fallen in love with. It was on the top floor of a four-story building and had a large front balcony bordered by all kinds of potted plants. On the kitchen fridge was a magnet from New College, the small school Geoffrey had attended in Florida. Most people have never heard of it, so the magnet felt like a friendly connection with these strangers. I could look out windows and see the top branches of trees, giving me the feeling that I was in the country instead of Chicago.

I called Wayne to let him know I had arrived and unpacked my suitcase. Then it was time to go to a welcome reception. I found the car in the garage behind the apartments, backed through the impossibly narrow door—just inches to spare on either side—and drove to the campus, hoping I wouldn't get lost. When I arrived, I breathed a sigh of relief and took a moment to gather my courage before I went in to meet faculty and fellow-students, a few women but mostly men. Following the reception, we students went out to dinner together, and I finally relaxed enough to have fun.

After my first day of classes, I called Wayne again. Much about the day had been hard. The still-new drive to school made me tense, and one class in particular overwhelmed me. It was a course in research methods, which turned out to be partly statistics. That was bad enough, but by the end of the term I would need to know the subject for my doctoral research project and to write an initial proposal. For some classmates, this was their second or third term, so they had been thinking and talking about their projects for months or even a year. For me, it was a new idea. The more the professor talked, the more distressed and despairing I felt. I didn't have a clue what I wanted to focus on or even the kind of topics people chose for research. I couldn't ask any questions because I knew if I did, my voice would quiver and I'd start to cry. I focused on getting through the class without crying.

As soon as I heard Wayne's voice on the phone that evening, I started to cry. "I don't think I can do this," I said through my tears—at least I could talk to him when I was crying. "We have to come up with a research project by the end of this session, and I don't even know where to start."

"You have three weeks," he said. "Don't feel like you need to know right away."

"Yes, but everyone else seems to know what they are doing."

"Surely your professor will give you some help in figuring it out."

"But I can't even talk to him about it right now. I'll start crying and feel like a fool."

"I'm sure he has talked with students who are upset before. Don't be so hard on yourself."

"He did suggest that we look at old projects," I conceded, "but I don't know where they are in the library . . . I just don't want to be here. I want to be home with you," I started to cry again. After a bit I calmed down and told him about the path around a little peninsula jutting into Lake Michigan where I had decided to walk every day. I also told him about the carefully-designed little Shakespeare garden with an arbor where I could sit and feel like I was in another world, even though I could hear the traffic on Sheridan Road. I felt better when I hung up.

The next day, Randy, one of my classmates, went with me to find the DMin projects in the library basement, and we looked at a number of them. I felt less alone. Randy became my closest friend. He told me that he had grown up Mennonite, in a different branch of the denomination than mine, but close enough for us to have some commonality in our background. He probably sensed how overwhelmed I felt and offered me companionship. He was a large person and his solid presence reassured me. He helped me persevere.

I did arrive at a project topic by the end of the three weeks. I would look at how men's shifting views of God to include female or feminine images affected their self-esteem. I had recently read a book about how women's self-esteem increased when they made that shift. I reasoned that the same would be true for men because they would no longer need to distance themselves from their feminine side and could be more whole. The idea had grown organically through my telling others about some of my experiences around images of God and listening to classmates' stories. By the end of the term, I had even been able to identify a list of resources.

When I returned the following January, Evanston was as cold and snowy as it had been hot and muggy in July, but this time I was in the dorm and began to feel more connected with the other women in the program. We got back our papers, and I discovered with relief that none of my professors questioned my ability to be there. The papers were ungraded, but they contained positive comments. However, I continued to resist the work I had to do. I found class discussion exhilarating, but I didn't feel the same about the papers. Was I just lazy, or were the assignments too complex for me?

Back home in Manassas, I attended a clergy women's group, but only one other woman, Kate, showed up. I had brought the book *Circle of Stones: Woman's Journey into Herself* by Judith Duerk to read a brief section as an opening for the meeting, so I read it to her.

> How might your life have been different, if . . . there had been a place for you, a place where you could go to be among women . . . when you had feelings of darkness? . . . And, what if, after that, every time you had feelings of darkness, you knew that [an older] woman would come to be with you? And would sit quietly by as you went into your darkness to listen to your feelings and bring them to birth . . . So that . . . you learned to no longer fear your darkness, but to trust it . . . to trust it as the place where you could meet your own deepest nature and give it voice.

This description became my experience that morning. I hadn't intended to talk about myself, but since it was just the two of us, I told Kate about my struggle with schoolwork and she listened—she simply listened—to my fears, my resistance, my anger, my darkness. She didn't argue any of it away, but after I had finished my litany of complaints, she began to question some of my statements and beliefs about myself. Were they really true? What did I get by seeing myself as limited and lacking?

She helped me face the reality that what I actually feared was my competence. I didn't want to acknowledge it because then I would have to take responsibility for it, and taking responsibility would mean doing hard work and taking uncomfortable risks. I did belong in this program. I had gotten here legitimately. I could do the work. I just didn't want to. I needed to face this challenge and whatever discomfort it brought—it was all a part of using the abilities I had been given.

Sitting with Kate, I experienced a conversion. What others might call my "conversion" at eight years old was not life-changing in the way this was. That had not been metanoia, a distinct turning around. I had simply taken the next step on a pathway I had been following. This was different. I made a conscious about-face, away from anger and fear toward acceptance and taking responsibility for the gifts and abilities I had been given.

From the outside things looked much the same. I was still going to school, doing the same work. My direction didn't appear to change, but a tectonic shift occurred within. I was no longer afraid. I knew I could do the tasks at hand. I might not be brilliant, but I was equal to what life required of me. This was a lesson I seemed to need to learn over and over again, but this time it stuck in a way it never had before. I ceased my struggling and resistance and simply faced my work.

It was summertime again in Evanston, the last session of my DMin classes. Every day was hot. Lake Michigan sparkled in the unremitting sun. The dorms were not air conditioned, though the late-night breezes brought slightly cooler air. We had classes all day long, five days of the week. I no longer questioned whether I should be there. I felt comfortable and part of the class, able to hold my own.

Yet it was with some trepidation that I went to my assessment tools class, where we had been looking at the results of the Minnesota Multiphasic Personality Inventory (MMPI) that we had each given to a client. Everyone in the class took the test as well, and I had asked the professor, John, to comment on our scores once we finished looking at our clients' profiles. I was curious what he would have to say but also anxious about having my personal foibles and dysfunctions spread over the board for everyone to see.

Mine was the last to be looked at, and, to my relief, it proved to be more interesting than embarrassing. At the end I thanked John for going over it. He responded that this was just part of his job. I countered by saying that it was an extra we had requested, and he retorted, "This is what you are paying me to do." I felt dismissed, but I let it go. During the break I kept pondering, trying to figure out what felt so wrong to me. One of the categories in the MMPI measures one's ability to maintain a persona, often seen as a dysfunction; but for clergy it can translate into the ability to keep clear boundaries between personal feelings and professional roles. It occurred to me that those two styles had just collided.

After the break, I voiced my observation: I had spoken from a personal, relational place, and John had maintained a professional stance. John responded to me, and we dived into an intense interchange about role playing and male-female dynamics. I was clear, passionate, and confident. There was none of the anxiety that often made me wordless or fuzzy-minded, trying to come up with responses as the other person spoke. My heart rate did not increase; my cheeks did not get red; I felt no uncomfortable intensity. I listened carefully and responded with words that flowed from somewhere deep within myself—unpremeditated words that came like the spring of water Jesus promised the Samaritan woman at the well, words about authenticity and the value of interacting openly with others, words about not hiding behind a wall of impersonal objectivity or hierarchical position. At one point, John asked me how I felt about the conversation, and after my response, he asked whether I was going to ask him how he felt. He told me he felt "enjoyment" in seeing me use my intellect. That angered me. He was treating me as if I were a wind-up toy to be observed. I pushed right back, wanting a personal interaction rather than him taking the stance of a patronizing observer.

Finally, he shifted. He began to speak personally, talking about his unease with boundaries, not always knowing where they were, and about his fear of being misunderstood. By then class time was nearly over. He asked my classmates, all of whom were men, how they felt about the interchange. One responded that it made him think of Jacob wrestling with the angel. Another said that he saw it as an interchange between two keen intellects. A third said he enjoyed how openly I had challenged John. At the end, John turned to me and said that he liked me, respected me, and enjoyed having me in his class. This felt personal, and I thanked him.

At lunch in the cafeteria, I joined the table of "demons," as other students referred to those of us in the DMin program. For the entire lunch my colleagues talked about what I had done in class. I was taken aback. I didn't feel so much that I had *done* something as that something had *emerged* from within me, something both familiar and also different. As they spoke on and on, I made one of my usual self-deprecatory comments. "You can't say that anymore," a classmate responded. "We saw you this morning. You are powerful and articulate. We won't let you pretend otherwise." I blushed, but I couldn't argue.

The next morning, I called Wayne. "Now I know why I had to do this program," I said, going on to tell him about my exchange with John. Wayne, as usual, said little by way of response, although I could tell by his voice that he was happy for me. I knew that he was also relieved that I would soon be home, and we could slip back into our normal routines.

37

Mother

LIFE WAS MOVING AT a fast pace, pulling me along. Classes were over, and I had begun work on my DMin project. Once started, I felt like a vehicle engaged in the tracks of a car wash, being pulled through at a pace I could not control. I had interviewed one of the persons whose story I would use for my research and had several more interviews set up.

In the meantime, I was preparing for our annual family trip to Charter Hall, a turn-of-the-century summer place set in a quiet inlet of the Chesapeake Bay. Our extended Lehman family gathered there for one idyllic weekend every August. The house itself sat in the shade of big, old oak, ash, and maple trees, while sunlight played off the water each day, creating a hundred different moods from morning to night. Most evenings we gathered on the dock to watch the glow of the sun fade away and stars appear. The cooler air whispered around us as birds finished their last chirping conversations of the day, and water lapped gently against the posts. I always looked forward to this relaxing prelude to the coming busy fall, but this year I yearned for it more than usual.

Both sons were home: Geoffrey, along with his girlfriend, from Boston and Jeremy from Philadelphia. All five of us could drive to Charter Hall in one car, a rare chance for us to be together. Then, several days before we were to leave, Mother called.

"Kathie, I've been thinking that if Esther and I drive to your place, we could ride with you from there to Charter Hall. I just don't have the energy to drive all that way."

"Mother, our car will be full. There are five of us, you know. We won't have room."

"Well, I guess that would mean going in two cars. I'm happy for someone to drive mine."

"Why can't you drive all the way?"

"I'm just not up to it, and I don't want Esther to drive. She gets flustered too easily."

"I know that, but I've been looking forward to the five of us riding together. We almost never have the chance to do something like this."

"I know. I'm sorry, Kathie, but I don't think I can do it."

"Mother, I don't understand. Just in June you drove twelve hours to Ontario and twelve hours back all by yourself, and that didn't seem to be a problem. Why can't you drive an hour and a half to Charter Hall?"

"I know. It doesn't make sense, but that's the way it is. If we can't go with you, I guess we'll just have to stay home. I hate to miss Charter Hall, but if we can't ride with you, I can't go."

"Well, OK. Let me think about it. Perhaps there is some other way . . . I'll call back later."

I hung up and turned to Wayne. "Mother wants to ride with us to Charter Hall," I said to him. "It just feels like one more attempt by her to be part of our family. I want to say no, but if she doesn't go, then I'll feel guilty . . . I get so tired of being put into these impossible situations. Why can't we do something on our own without her needing to be a part of it?"

"I don't know what you should do," he responded. "You'll have to figure that out. Either way is fine to me."

I stewed. I had been working at being clear and more assertive with Mother, saying what I wanted rather than acquiescing to such requests out of my need not to hurt her and then finding myself churning with resentment. I felt in a bind. I had heard sadness in her voice, and I knew she looked forward to the weekend as much as I did. Maybe if we waited a day or two, things would work themselves out.

She called again the next day. "Kathie, I just came home from the doctor's office," she said. She had a blood disorder related to platelets that her doctor monitored, but she had decided to see him ahead of schedule. "He ordered a blood test but also did a bone marrow biopsy."

"A bone marrow biopsy?" My heart did a flip—that wasn't normal.

"Yes. And it really hurt. The results will be in tomorrow. The doctor thinks I have leukemia."

"Leukemia? Really?" I could hear the fear and vulnerability in her voice, and I felt myself melting, wanting to hold my fragile little mother in my arms.

"Well, I hope he is wrong, I really do." I was no longer fighting against my desire to protect her. I felt only numb denial. "Mother, I love you and want you to be around for a long time yet."

"So do I, but this is in God's hands."

I hung up the receiver. How could this be? Mother with leukemia? At Christmastime she had a cold that lingered for weeks and I was concerned, but she had finally gotten over it and seemed well. She drove to Ontario to visit Carol in June and reported a good trip. A few weekends earlier we had gone to help her clean out her attic because she was thinking of moving to a cottage in the retirement community just blocks from her house. She seemed fine then and had even made an apple pie especially for me.

The next evening Mother called again to say that she had acute myeloid leukemia. Aunt Dot, who was visiting in Harrisonburg, had gone along with her to the doctor's office and had taken notes on everything. The doctor said he did not recommend chemotherapy for anyone over sixty-five because only one in ten survive it. Mother was nearly seventy-five. The only treatment option was blood transfusions, and they would work only so long. There was no cure. He said she probably had two to three months to live. I wrote in my journal:

> I can't really comprehend yet what is happening. My mind seems slow and dim-witted and unwilling to move in the direction of Mother [being] sick and dying. She so much wants to live . . . What I have felt most about my mother is her vulnerability. I've seen her courage and her vast love for life, for travel, for her family. But what I have *felt* has been her pain, her longings, and her sense of being at the bottom of the power structures in her community and family.

Mother was powerless to change her disease, and once again, I was powerless to make it better for her. There was no further debate about rides to Charter Hall. We would go in two cars.

When she and Aunt Esther arrived on Friday morning, we packed the cars as if everything were perfectly normal. The task at hand was getting to Charter Hall. I drove one car with all the women, and Wayne and our sons went in the other car. Our usual carefree weekend was weighed down with heaviness, although we managed to have an early birthday celebration for Mother. We sang hymns together Sunday morning as we always did.

The last time our family was all together—several weeks before Mother's death. *Left to right:* **Carol, me, Mother, and Jeanie.**

The following week, Carol and her family came from Canada to visit Mother. Jeanie already lived in Harrisonburg, and our family came from Manassas for the weekend. Mother was tired and made no attempt to help with any of the meals, nor did she join in any of the games, although she was usually one of the most enthusiastic players. On Sunday morning we sat in the living room and talked about the coming months—who would be given power of attorney, what she wanted for her funeral, whether any of us would want to buy her house, who would get certain pieces of furniture, when each of us could be there to help. We took lots of pictures in various groupings, knowing this was probably the last time we would all be together.

Back home I began making arrangements to take off blocks of time from work. Mother's illness increased at an alarming rate; her white blood count went from 38,000 to 52,000 to 76,000 in one week, with a normal range being 4,500 to 10,000. At 98,000 something catastrophic could happen at any moment, the doctor told us. I drove the two hours to Harrisonburg for planned times and unplanned ones as well. One evening I left Manassas in a hurry, letting Wayne take over stirring the batch of peach jam on the stove, because Jeanie called to say Mother had been extremely lethargic all day. I arrived at 10:00 p.m. By then, she was feeling better and the three of us sat and talked until late. The next morning, I looked out the front window and was surprised to see Aunt Dot walking across the front lawn. She and Uncle Bob, who had returned to Indiana after Charter Hall, had driven through the night to be there again. I was relieved to have my aunt's capable nursing skills on hand and to have someone older to turn to. Aunt Esther's memory had begun to slip.

That Sunday afternoon, in a rare interlude, I sat with Mother as she napped on the living room sofa. I reflected on our relationship, writing,

> Being here . . . feels like the "wonderful one-hoss shay" [that lasted 100 years and then fell apart all at once]. Everything is going—her fridge is on its last leg, a burner on the stove doesn't work, . . . towels are threadbare and frazzled, her fan doesn't work right, the lampshade . . . has a hole in it, . . . her piano is out of tune, her living room furniture is worn, and her sweeper has no suction.
>
> Her life has been full, well-used, and perhaps ready to be traded in for something better. Her tired disappointments and frustrations can be laid aside for a new kind of health and strength.
>
> She keeps talking about the *power* of God. It feels to me like she places all power outside herself. I see it so painfully clearly because that is what she taught me too. All power is too extreme, but not by much. There is a lot of power in her that is hard for her to grasp.
>
> Mother looks at me with such love and joy in her eyes and tells me how happy she is that I can be here. I feel her love and her dearness and her deep joy in life. In some ways we are so alike and in other ways so different, much more alike than I want to recognize. I like the times when she and I are alone. It still feels like competition for her attention when C and J are around, not that they are aware of competing, but that they fill the space.
>
> That is how I give my power away—letting myself feel without power. Neither Carol or Jeanie struggle in the same way I do. They are much faster to demand their rights. [In contrast] Mother and I have a way of quietly persevering that is unlike their more assertive style.

We celebrated Mother's seventy-fifth birthday on August 28. Carol had gone home and was back again, this time to stay as long as needed. Only a few days later came an evening of intense pain for Mother, and the hospice nurse gave her morphine, which led to a coma. "She will most likely be like this for a number of days," the nurse told us, so I went home to do a scheduled interview for my doctoral project the following day. When the phone rang at 3:00 a.m., I knew what it was before Wayne answered. Mother was gone. We hurriedly repacked our things and drove to Harrisonburg in record time on empty pre-dawn roads. Jeanie met me at the door with a hug. When I walked into the bedroom where Mother's body lay, Carol was sitting there holding her hand. She stood up and said, "Here, hold Mother's hand. We've kept it warm for you."

Mother had planned her funeral, but we three sisters planned the burial of her ashes. The cemetery agreed to dig a foot-deep grave directly above Papa's much deeper grave. On a clear September day, I stood and looked around me at the late-summer fields. Off to the side, Mole Hill, an ancient volcanic plug now covered with trees, rose from the valley floor with near-perfect breast-like symmetry. To the east stood the faithful Massanutten Peak with a line of more distant blue mountains extending beyond it. Cicadas and crickets maintained a constant chatter while birds sang overtime, as if trying to get in extra songs before cold weather came. The sun shone warmly on our small gathering of family and close friends. Mother would have exulted in this perfect late-summer day. I could feel her joy and was grateful that she could be laid to rest here in the midst of such quiet beauty.

I led the short service and framed it around the image of tucking Mother into her resting place as she had tucked us into bed when we were young. First, we lined the shallow grave with flowers and greenery. Wayne dropped in a Junket tablet, a bit of rennet to represent all the homemade ice cream events we had shared over the years. Lyle, Carol's husband, gently placed a song sparrow's nest along with that, and Carol's little six-year-old Myra solemnly dropped in some favorite "buddons" (buttons) from a made-up game she played with Mother. Then each of us daughters, followed by our children, spread her ashes. We sang songs and told stories as she had done for us, before covering her with a blanket of soil. Carol led the songs, and Jeanie read scripture. We cried and laughed and talked about what we would miss the most. Then we drove away, leaving her last physical remnants behind in the warm Virginia soil she had loved with such a passion.

It was Friday evening, the end of the week. I stood at the stove sautéing onions when Wayne came in, having stopped at the bank on the way home from work to pick up some final checks. He had been appointed Mother's executor, and it had taken a year to dispense with her modest estate. He was finally finished. He went into the dining room and moments later called me to come. I turned off the burner and wiped my hands on my apron as I went. There, laid out on the table, were all the addressed envelopes containing checks to the people and organizations to whom Mother had left her money. He showed me the cashier's checks he had just gotten for Geoffrey and Jeremy. I first looked at their names and thought about what it would feel like for them to get these checks and then I saw "Estate of Miriam L. Weaver" on the signature line and was overcome. Wayne, who was so pleased to finally complete this complicated task, put his arms around me and let me cry. I felt not only sad but desperate, as I had felt many years ago when Mother was about to separate her paper doll family. But this time, rather than keeping paper dolls together, I wanted to tear up all the checks into impossibly small pieces and make them disappear. I wanted Mother to be in her kitchen on College Avenue, heating up leftover meat loaf and cooking her dozen lima beans, carefully doled out from the produce of her small garden. It took a little while before I was able to tell Wayne what I was feeling.

The task of the evening would be to mail all these neatly addressed envelopes. I still had Friday night work to do—laundry to fold and supper to finish. As I knelt at the sofa folding towels, I startled myself by saying, "I want to go out and get drunk tonight, so drunk I can't think"—something I had never done. Instead, I called my friend Sandy and asked if she and her husband Dexter would like to meet us at a nearby café after we mailed the checks.

Wayne and I got through supper and washed the dishes, and then I could put off this task no longer. We drove the short distance to the post office, where Wayne handed me the envelopes to mail. For a moment I wanted him to go along, but I quickly changed my mind. This was something I needed to do alone.

No one else was in the post office, to my relief. I stood at the mail slot and put in one envelope at a time, noting the name of each recipient and Mother's relationship to them. The collection represented significant aspects of her life: her three daughters; her three grandchildren; Mennonite Central Committee, where she had had her first secretarial job; Eastern Mennonite University, where she studied and taught; Virginia Mennonite Mission Board, under which she and Papa had gone to Kentucky; Mennonite Mutual Aid, on whose board she had served for many years.

I came out crying and cried all the way to the café. Then I dried my eyes and went in to meet our friends. I found the most decadent chocolate confection on the menu to go with my coffee, and although Sandy and Dexter knew what I had just done, we didn't talk about it. Instead we talked about our children and laughed and told jokes. I had spent all my tears for that day and now reveled in the rich comfort of good food and even better friends who could be with me in sorrow while allowing joy as well.

38

Becoming Trunkie

I STEERED WAYNE TO the right floor and room in the Garrett dormitory, where we were to spend the night. We had just arrived from O'Hare Airport and had picked up a key to get into the locked building. My graduation was the next day. I was excited and could hardly believe that I would now be finished with school. It had been fourteen years since I had taken my first graduate-level class, and it seemed ages ago. In the previous year and a half, I had interviewed research subjects and written a research paper. Only months earlier, I made a quick trip to Garrett to defend it.

My joy about graduation was tempered by the fact that Mother wasn't there. She had been gone less than a year, and I still felt her absence keenly. But tonight, my excitement and joy took second seat to my puzzlement. Wayne kept doing strange things and wouldn't tell me why. He had rushed me through dinner, although we had nothing else to do that evening. As soon as we got to the dorm, he went to the restroom and didn't come back for twenty or twenty-five minutes. I asked if he wasn't feeling well. He felt fine. Did he get lost finding the restroom designated for men on the floor above us? Not really. He couldn't say what took him so long. Then he couldn't get done fixing the screen in our open window. I told him it would be OK the way it was, but he kept fiddling. He had to go to the bathroom again and was gone equally long. When I questioned him, he gave vague answers and said he'd explain later. I didn't understand why he couldn't just tell me. I finally gave up and got into my nightgown, but he went out again. Just as I was ready to crawl into bed, I heard a light tap at the door. Before I got to it, the door opened and there stood Carol, with Wayne hovering in the background. "Carol!" I exclaimed. She was grinning. I opened my arms and we hugged, half laughing, half crying. "How in the world did you get here? I asked.

The newly minted Reverend Doctor Kathleen Weaver Kurtz.

"I flew. How do you think?" she said, still teary. "I was supposed to get here before dark, but my plane was delayed and I had no way to let Wayne know."

"I knew she didn't know where to come, and the office was closed and the building locked," Wayne said, "so I had to keep inventing ways to watch for her." Their explanations tumbled over each other, and Wayne's strange behavior finally made sense.

I quickly dressed again while Carol put her things in her room, and then we went out to find something for her to eat. As we walked across campus, she said that she wanted to surprise me, knowing that Mother wouldn't be there. She and Wayne had plotted together during her last visit. I remembered coming into the kitchen one day while they were doing dishes together and being aware that a conversation had ended abruptly, but I had thought little of it at the time. This is what they had been talking about.

The next day, Friday, I graduated, and after a luncheon for graduates and their families, I showed Wayne and Carol around the campus. We spent Saturday wandering from venue to venue at the annual Chicago Blues Festival, listening to various performers. I felt freer than I had in a long time.

Back home in Virginia, I barely paused before beginning the two remaining tasks I had set myself for the year. I wanted to be done. I couldn't fully enjoy my freedom until I had finished hoop-jumping. My first task was doing paperwork to move from member to fellow—the level for established therapists—in the American Association of Pastoral Counselors (AAPC). This was not difficult, just a matter of getting together the documents and evaluations required. The other task was much more daunting: studying for the state licensure exam, which would be given in October. I listened to tutorial tapes, worked through a study manual, doubled up supervision sessions to get in the required number of hours, and took practice exams. My goal was not high. Passing would do.

I went to Richmond to take the pencil and paper test, which then took weeks to meander through the slow channels of being scored. Finally, the week before Christmas, on a morning when everyone else had gone shopping, the envelope arrived. I recognized what it was before I opened it and sat down at the kitchen table—the same table where, many years before, I had read Walter Wink's book and wrote that I wanted to study theology and Carl Jung. I slit the envelope, took a deep breath, and pulled out the single sheet that informed me that I had passed with a few points to spare.

Now I was surely done—doctor of ministry degree, AAPC fellow, state licensure. Work always held challenges, but I had reached my goal. There was a part of myself that could relax and stop pushing so hard. I could finally feel settled, if not actually coast.

Then the organization where I worked needed another person who would be able to offer supervision to newer staff members. To my surprise, Becky (my former therapist) suggested that I would be good at that. I had never considered becoming a supervisor for all my usual reasons. However, it didn't take long for me to decide to give it a try. I had worked enough years to meet state supervision qualifications, so I began supervising one person and then another.

About a year later, our organization began a residency in pastoral counseling. Doug, one of my colleagues, set up the program, and I was chosen to co-lead. Together we supervised and taught a group of residents. It seemed so natural that I soon forgot I had ever questioned it.

Doug was always challenging himself—a grueling "Bike across America" ride, a new therapy technique, a triathlon. He began talking about moving to the diplomate level in the AAPC, the level for supervisors. I passed it off as his next challenge. I admired his confidence, maybe even felt a little envious, but diplomate level was for those at the top, not me.

Then one day Doug said to me, "Kathie, I think you should do this too." I felt the familiar thud in my stomach and responded without a pause, "Oh, I couldn't do that." This was still my automatic response, even though I *knew* better. I didn't think about it again until that night in bed when I remembered our conversation. I dismissed it again, not wanting to lie awake and face my fear. The next day as I drove to work Doug's words came back to me. Clearly this wasn't going away. What would be the harm in taking the required course? It could be helpful for both Doug and me to take it since we supervised together. I could decide later whether or not to finish the diplomate process. I'll take the class, I thought, feeling both lighter and scared.

Doug and I flew to Louisville for the class. This time, at least, I wasn't going alone to a new place. As usual, I found that I did fit into the group and could hold my own with people who turned out to be a lot like me. I actually enjoyed it. Inspired by the course, I decided to do the required fifty hours of supervision of my work, even though it meant a two-hour drive each way twice a month. Diplomate supervisors were hard to find. Before I knew it, I was relenting completely. If I took the class and did the supervision, I may as well write the paper, gather a portfolio of my writings and presentations, and have the interview. Once started, I might as well finish, even though I was within a decade of retirement. Part of me wondered if it was really worth my effort, but I discovered that the writing process enabled me to integrate my years of learning and experience in a way that nothing else could have done. Its value lay in helping me see the way my path had branched off again and again, taking me to places I hadn't intended, places beyond any dreams I had for myself. In Rosamond's words, I had pushed out the walls of the chapel. My world had enlarged—or perhaps I had just allowed myself to grow into the world that was there all the time, waiting for me to move from the fog of my fears out into the bright clarity of day.

❦

Our organization's outreach coordinator came to speak to the counseling residents about building caseloads. The first thing she did was ask each person to draw a tree that represented how they saw themselves professionally at that point. Doug and I participated in the activity.

I have always loved trees—their greenness, their arching branches, the flexibility that enables even sturdy trunks to move with the wind. I thought of the maples around Grandpa's house and the sycamores along Catron Creek. Reaching for a crayon, I began to draw my tree with branches reaching off the top of the sheet, and roots running off the bottom. I was not inclined to add any blossoms, fruit, or wildlife, but I took time to try to make the bark look as realistic as I could.

We started around the group, each resident describing their picture. Some were artfully drawn. Some had fruit in the branches or birds resting there. I glanced at my tree and realized that I hadn't actually drawn a whole tree. Most of the picture was tree trunk. What did that mean, I asked myself? Then it was my turn. I began a bit apologetically, "I guess I am feeling trunkie today." Everybody laughed. I went on to observe that the trunk is the center of energy and gravity for a tree, connecting the roots and branches to each other. This represents the way I see my role as a supervisor, I explained, providing a connection between past traditions and emerging practice. My comments surprised me because I had been thinking none of that as I drew. Only after class did it occur to me how literally true this was.

The concept of providing pastoral care has existed for thousands of years, but pastoral counseling as a formal discipline began only a century ago, largely through the work of Anton Boisen. Through his own struggles with schizophrenia, he became interested in the spiritual experiences of people who have mental illness. His life's work became the exploration of how spiritual meaning emerges through mental and emotional problems. He created structures within medical settings to offer spiritual and religious support to patients. Out of the work he and his students did emerged two branches of caregiving: chaplaincy and pastoral counseling.

I was only two or three degrees away from Boisen. When I had gone to hear Wayne Oates speak at a conference during my Chambersburg years, I was listening to one of Boisen's students. During seminary, I had done a summer of chaplaincy training at St. Elizabeths Hospital in a program established by Ernie Bruder, another of Boisen's students.

And yet another of Boisen's students, Carroll Wise, had taught several of my teachers.

Now I was teaching residents studying pastoral care. They were the leafing branches, producing the new, green growth that would add new twigs and leaves to the field. My role was to keep them grounded and connected to the tradition as I supported their growth, branching out to places I would never go. It was appropriate that my drawing was about the trunk of the tree. I *was* trunkie.

39

Closing the Circle

THE RECEPTION HAD BARELY begun. Radell and Sarah were properly married and the room full of wedding attendees, some of them Weaver cousins, settled into happy conversation. Just under the buzz of dozens of voices, I heard my phone's single ding, informing me that I had a text. I pulled the phone from my purse as unobtrusively as I could and glanced at it under the table. "Congratulations," the message began. It couldn't be. I hastily read the rest of the message. "Wayne!" I said holding out the phone for him to see: "Congratulations, your offer on the house has been accepted!" It was our real estate agent, to whom Wayne had just sent the last bank document minutes before we left for the wedding. My eyes filled with tears. The beautiful house in Harrisonburg we had looked at Friday afternoon, the one that had almost none of our practical requirements, was going to be ours! I could hardly believe it.

Wayne and I were both retired and had decided to move back to Harrisonburg, back to the place where I had grown up. We had been looking at houses for months and then made an uncharacteristic, on-the-spot decision. The house we had looked at the day before did not have a first-floor bedroom or laundry or a garage, but Wayne had fallen in love with the little den and the screened-in porch. I had breathed in a sigh of contentment when I walked into the living room, with its wide expanse of gleaming hardwood floor and triple windows framing a huge magnolia tree—a luxurious treehouse of a room. I liked the curve of the hallway bannister and the large master bedroom. We discussed workarounds for its lacks. The agent told us that two other parties were interested in the house and we probably needed to decide by morning. My heart sank. I didn't want to get into a bidding war, and I also wanted time to consider this major decision. "Let me know by morning," she said.

We went to a restaurant for dinner, and our food had just been served when Wayne's phone rang. It was our agent saying two offers had been made, and if we wanted to be in the running, we needed to make our offer later that evening. No time for careful deliberation or agonizing over our list of priorities. We said we'd meet her at the office in an hour. It felt like a futile exercise to me. What chance did we have with two other interested parties?

That night I tried to let go of the outcome. I reiterated all the reasons the house would not work. I told myself that we still had time to find another. But mostly I thought of the oak floors and big windows and screened-in porch.

Now it was to be ours. On our way home from the wedding reception, we stopped again to see what we had agreed to. This time we walked around the backyard where daffodils—more varieties than I had ever grown—were in full bloom. I began picking a bouquet. These were almost mine. No one lived in the house, so no one else would be picking them or looking out the windows to enjoy them. Why not take some home with me as a promise of more to come?

We were startled by the rush of a small dog, yapping and running back and forth sniffing first one and then the other of us. "Ziggy, come here," yelled a man from the next yard, but Ziggy, being more curious than obedient continued his frenetic circling. The man came into the yard, introduced himself as Dany and asked if we had bought the house. He welcomed us and explained that this neighborhood had been developed by a group of families who were friends and wanted to live near each other. He and his family were living in the house his mother had built. The neighbor across the street was also living in her mother's house. This was a real neighborhood.

Driving back to Manassas gave us time to ponder our sudden change. In twenty-four hours, we had gone from frustration to love at first sight. I had resisted looking at the house because it didn't meet our requirements, but Wayne had wanted to see it. We would be in Harrisonburg for the wedding, so we might as well look. I had been prepared to add it to the long list of houses that we had rejected. And I had been surprised.

The return to Harrisonburg had become real. But was I really returning home? Park View was no longer the Mennonite enclave it had been in the 1950s and 1960s. It had been incorporated into Harrisonburg sometime after I left home, but now even the streets that had been "non-Mennonite" in my childhood were liberally spotted with the three-colored signs welcoming neighbors in Spanish, English, and Arabic—signs that originated here in a Mennonite congregation. Boundaries were blurred.

I played one of my favorite "what if" games, imagining my younger, college-age self, driving along Myers Avenue, seeing the new Cape Cod house sitting low on the hillside, and being told that this house will one day be mine—this house in "secular" Harrisonburg. What would I have thought? I would have had trouble believing that I'd live in such a trim-looking house. I would have wondered why I'd chosen to live here, outside my own community, and been amazed that such a move might feel natural rather than a venture into a foreign place where I wouldn't fit in.

Taking the game one step further, I imagined being given a résumé of the self now buying the house. Would I have recognized in her the Kathie that I knew then? The elementary school teacher part would not have surprised me, and the years in Botswana would have fit within my imagined life, but beyond that was foreign territory—unimaginable—because I didn't know such things could be coupled with my name. The idea of graduating from seminary or being a pastor would not have crossed my mind. The little I knew of counselors was surrounded by mystique. The initials after my name would have been a foreign language.

In the coming days those musings dissolved into a whirlwind of activity. Finding a contractor to do renovations; choosing paint colors, new kitchen cabinets, flooring, and fixtures; ordering a new furnace; arranging for deck repairs—the list seemed endless and my energy less so. We were also readying our old house to go on the market. The summer became a blur of trips between Manassas and Harrisonburg. We said goodbye to Northern Virginia friends and made contact in Harrisonburg with friends from earlier parts of our lives.

Finally, the summer ended. One rainy afternoon we sat on the floor of our completely emptied house in Manassas eating cheese and crackers after the last helpers left. I had one more floor to wash and then we would lock the house and leave it forever. We didn't talk. We were too tired and overwhelmed. I didn't feel much other than exhaustion and the necessity of keeping on moving. I grudgingly got up, filled a bucket with water, and willed my already sore knees to wash one last floor. I thought of all the feet that had walked that floor over the past thirty-four years—family no longer living, my sons' ex-girlfriends of whom I'd been fond, work colleagues, beloved daughters-in-law, grandchildren's toddling feet, women's groups, cousins and their families. Those times were all past. Even if I stayed in the house, I couldn't retrieve them, but leaving made the memories feel more distant and bittersweet.

With the last floor clean, I took my cell phone and made a slow video tour through the house, thinking how lucky the people were who would be coming in, and feeling in some hazy corner that I really wanted to move right back into this well-cleaned, inviting place. I hoped I would grow to love our new house as deeply. There weren't any tears, because I needed to keep going. Besides, my mind was full of things to remember to do when we got to Harrisonburg, where Jeanie would welcome us, feed us, and give us a night of rest before moving in began; where Lois—yes, the hard-boiled-eggs-for-lunch Lois from first grade—would come to clean a cupboard for us; and where friends from our Harlan days who were living nearby would bring us a meal.

By Christmastime, our house had begun to feel like home. We decided to have a Christmas story party like the ones we had in Manassas for many years. Story parties had been part of my growing up. Every year at Christmas, the Sarco family invited their nearby Park View neighbors for an evening of listening to stories or an entire book being read. Afterward we had cookies and punch. It was an evening my sisters and I looked forward to. Wayne and I had done a similar thing in Manassas, asking a friend to read for a mix of church, community, and work friends. It was a tradition I wanted to continue in our new setting, bringing it back to the community where it had begun. Limiting the guest list to what our living and dining room would hold presented a challenge. Surely, they won't all come, I thought, as I added a few more and a few more names to the list, but nearly all of them did, so we scrunched in. I asked Jay Landis, a favorite high school English teacher and family friend who had read at some of those childhood story parties, to be our reader.

When everyone was settled and the story began, I looked over the room and realized what a cross-section of my life was represented there: among those gathered were school friends from first grade through college and old Park View neighbors, as well as friends from our days in Botswana, Harlan, Chambersburg, and Manassas. We had family with us too: my sister Jeanie and some Weaver and Lehman cousins. I had moved back into the history of my life, but I wasn't the same person who had left. I had ventured out into worlds I had never envisioned for myself—worlds of learning, of arts and new cultures, of different faith traditions. These had opened and enriched my life in countless ways.

For years I had resisted moving back to Harrisonburg, mainly afraid that I would feel constricted there by family expectations and a community that still clung to beliefs that no longer fit me. Now I was clear and confident enough in who I had become that I no longer feared that old expectations would limit me. I could bring my enlarged world with me. The friends who were wedged in on sofas and chairs represented the communities that had challenged and supported me in breaking through the barriers that were often as much self-imposed as real. They had also grown. The journey of life opens us all to wider vistas and deeper participation in the world, if we allow it to. I was home not because I was back where I grew up, but because I had come home to myself.

Coasting still is not an option. Challenges continue. Fear and shame, grief and discouragement, illness, disappointment, and death weave in and out. The stammering girl at the mic still tugs on my pant leg occasionally, warning me how scary it can be to speak. The fearful fledgling on the edge of the nest sometimes hesitates. But I have learned to speak with confidence, and I have found my wings. My long, anxiety-laden pregnancy has brought forth abundant life.

The blistering morning mist still swirls beyond the door, but the valley has opened up and my house is no longer small, no longer a prim square. It is a mansion with wide, open rooms, curious dormers poking out, more than one tower thrown up in a moment of exhilaration. There are new cellars dug into the clay and rocky soil beneath me. Windows abound, big ones, more than I can count. The roads I have traveled to get here have never been straight, and the ones leading on are no different. They curve and circle back around in scary, boring, tantalizing, glorious, inevitable loops through mists and clear skies. Some loops are large; others so small I don't see that I'm moving at all. And there is grace, everywhere—inside and out, swirling in the mist, gentling the curves of the road, focusing the light. It shapes the rocks that sometimes support, sometimes block, sometimes break apart before giving way to something new. Grace penetrates the blistering mist and shimmers in the sunlight, reminding me there is always more.

Wayne and me on our fiftieth wedding anniversary, December 2019.

Made in the USA
Middletown, DE
01 November 2021

51486443R00130